James Leatham

Socialism and Character

A Contribution Towards a System of Applied Ethics

James Leatham

Socialism and Character
A Contribution Towards a System of Applied Ethics

ISBN/EAN: 9783337009083

Printed in Europe, USA, Canada, Australia, Japan

Cover: Foto ©Thomas Meinert / pixelio.de

More available books at **www.hansebooks.com**

SOCIALISM & CHARACTER.

A CONTRIBUTION TOWARDS A SYSTEM OF
APPLIED ETHICS.

BY

JAMES LEATHAM.

Author of " The Class War," " Was Jesus a Socialist ? " etc.

—————

London :

THE TWENTIETH CENTURY PRESS, LIMITED,

37A, CLERKENWELL GREEN, E.C.

1897.

CONTENTS.

	PAGE.
PREFACE	V
THE NEED OF A SYSTEM OF ETHICS . .	I
THE PARTICULAR AND THE GENERAL .	14
HAS THE INDIVIDUAL A RIGHT TO HIMSELF? .	19
"THE CLEANLINESS OF THE SEXES"	27
THE ORIGIN OF ETHICS . .	39
CHARITY . . .	45
CHEERFULNESS . .	54
COURAGE . .	64
TRUTHFULNESS . .	77
HONESTY .	87
DILIGENCE . .	97
PUBLIC SPIRIT . .	117
PRESENT POSSIBILITIES OF MORAL IMPROVEMENT	141
APPENDIX—	
A.—BAIN ON THE STERILITY OF ABSTRACT PRINCIPLES IN ETHICS .	169
B.—THE SUBJECTION OF WOMEN .	171

" Morality must be considered as independent [of theology] and exclusively human in its origin."

" Moral right and wrong is not so much a simple indivisible property as an extensive code of regulations, which cannot even be understood without a certain maturity of intelligence."

— BAIN

PREFACE.

THE occasional spectacle of great devotion to the public good sometimes inclines one to think that faith is not so much dead as that the form of it has merely changed ; that it is now social instead of religious ; that whereas men formerly believed in a Moral Governor of the universe whom they could not see, and a future life of which they did not know, they now believe in the advent of a great Social Revolution in spite of many and disheartening evidences of the slowness of social progress. But this devotion to the public good is confined to a comparative few ; the generations now living do not generally deserve any credit for it ; and it springs not so much from faith as from confidence. Faith implies an element of credulity : it is belief without evidence, belief held sometimes contrary to the believer's experience. But the belief in a great social future and its near advent may be a reasoned and reasonable one. The progress made in the past is a guarantee of progress in the future ; and the belief in a Social Revolution becomes certainty when we see how little the present system has to offer to the self-interest of those who hold the vast preponderance of political power. The assumption running

through the following chapters—that in the future
society the Social-Democratic principle will play a
prime part in determining the relations of life—is
surely well warranted by the tendencies manifestly
at work in the body social to-day. No exercise of
faith is required for belief in the advent of Socialism;
for Socialism is admitted to be inevitable, even by
those who abhor it and dread its coming.

But faith, properly so-called, is dead. The belief
in God, with all it implies, is now without a *raison
d'être*. The original conception of God has everywhere been that of a Creator, a great Master Workman of the Universe, who made it and who sustains
it. But the idea of creation is now given up. The
conception of a universe beginning to be out of
nothing is found, even by Roman Catholic theo-
logians, to be unthinkable, and they now speak of
God and the Universe as "co-existent eternities."
This is certainly giving away the idea of God as the
Creator. Napoleon's triumphant, and as he fancied
conclusive, question regarding the starry firmament—
" Who made all that ?"—is answered by the theo-
logians themselves, and they say, " It never was
made: it existed from all eternity." The logical
corollary to the law of the indestructibility of matter
is its uncreatability, its unincreasableness.

Nor is the conception of God the Sustainer any
longer an intellectual necessity, as it was when men

could not account for the phenomena of Nature in terms of the natural. We know why the wind blows; why it rained yesterday and is fine to-day. We can assign the natural causes by which all changes take place in earth and air, in sea and sky. In every branch of cosmic activity we find cause producing effect, the effect serving in turn as the cause of some further effect, and nothing being lost in the transmission of either matter or force. In this circularity of phenomena, this endless chain of causation, there is no supernatural link, nothing that requires the intervention of an outside, independent First Cause. There is nothing left for Deity to do. His function and personality have, as Mark Pattison said, been "defecated to a pure transparency."

Many who feel the intellectual necessity of Atheism, and who are practically Atheists in the sense that God and Godism are utterly divorced from their life and thoughts, still cling, when pressed, to a sort of "profession of belief," because, as they imagine, morality cannot live save on the supposition of its Divine origin. The purpose of these pages is to show that morality is social and secular in its origin; that the strongest arguments for good conduct arise from its utility, necessity, and attractiveness in everyday life; and that it will be profoundly altered for the better by the conditions of life in the Social-Democratic State.

I do not know of any work on the same lines. I
have tried to be both concrete and constructive,
believing that the best way to expel anti-social
tendencies in thought and action is to instil pro-social
ideas and give the reasons for pro-social conduct.
As Comte said, "Nothing is destroyed until it is
replaced"; and the Vandals are out in such numbers,
and their blows fall with such vigour on the fabric
of conventional morality, that some replacement does
indeed require to be done.

Those who read these papers as they appeared
week by week in *Justice* will perhaps notice that the
chapter on the drink question has been omitted, as
well as the portion of the second chapter leading
up to it. This has been done, not because of any
material change of opinion on the question, but
because such a topic was apart from the constructive
aim and character of the book.   J. L.

MANCHESTER, 1897.

SOCIALISM AND CHARACTER.

A CONTRIBUTION TOWARDS A SYSTEM OF APPLIED ETHICS.

CHAPTER I.

THE NEED OF A SYSTEM OF ETHICS.

" Many persons who have given up the conventional *bourgeois* morality have not assimilated a Socialist morality, and hence have no morality at all. Their case is analogous to that of the savage who, under the instruction of the missionary, has learnt to despise the traditional and customary ethics of his tribe as heathen, and, having imperfectly understood the Christo-bourgeois mixture dealt out to him by the broadcloth man of God, has developed into as ill-conditioned a scoundrel as it is easy to meet."— E. BELFORT BAX.

THOSE who are fond of defining Socialism as a proposition in economics, or as a constitutional change, and who think that Socialists should confine their attention to subjects of an industrial, economic, or political kind, will probably disagree with much of what I have to say here. They may hold that there is no ethical system peculiar to Socialism ; that Socialists neither need nor want a new moral code ; that the Ten Commandments and the Golden Rule, if applied, are quite good enough for all Socialist

B

purposes. They may argue, in effect, that Socialism
is the revolt of the hungry, and that there is no reason
why a hungry Christian should not rebel as readily as
a hungry Atheist against the condition that entail
privation upon him. Plausible as this latter contention may seem, we find it controverted by the, I
should think, universal experience of those who have
been any length of time in the Socialist movement.
We do not often find the Christian proletaire rebelling
politically against unjust conditions of life. But
when occasionally he does, it will usually be found
that his Christianity—his other worldliness—suffers
in proportion as politics engage his attention. In the
course of a ten years' experience of the Socialist
movement in different parts of the country, I have
known cases of Quakers, Plymouth Brethren, and
even Roman Catholics joining our movement just
because they cherished devoutly the best tenets—that
is to say, the social and secular tenets—of their religion ; and these have, without exception, gradually
lost their interest in the existence of another world as
they became satisfied of the possibility of an ideal life
in this. Be the causes of the change what they may,
the fact that such a change takes place is undeniable.
At the present moment I cannot remember a single
instance of a person who is at one and the same time
a really earnest and intelligent Socialist and an ortho-
dox Christian. Those who do not openly attack the
Church and the fabric of Christianity show but scant
respect to either the one or the other in private, and
are always much less interested in their theology than
in their politics and economics. And while all of us

are thus indifferent to the Church, many of us are frankly hostile to her. Marx, Lassalle, and Engels, among earlier Socialists; Morris, Bax, Hyndman, Guesde, and Bebel, among present-day Socialists— are all more or less avowed Atheists: and what is true of the more notable men of the party is almost equally true of the rank and file the world over. Gronlund and Bellamy are notable examples to the contrary; but Bellamy can hardly be said to be in the move- ment; and Gronlund's Theism is so unlike that of the average Christian that he may fairly be claimed as one of the Pagans. At any rate, he is with the secular moralists in this—that he believes morality will be radically altered for the better by the conditions of life in the Co-operative Commonwealth.

But the necessity of showing in detail the secular basis of ethics arises, not alone from the fact the Biblical morals as such have no hold on the minds of Socialists, but also because they have no hold on the mass of mankind in professedly Christian countries. The average man of to-day may be nominally a Catholic or a Protestant, but he is in reality an Atheist in the strict, etymological meaning of the term —that is, one without God. Atheist as I am, I find myself appalled at the gross, contented, intellectually-dishonest irreligion—" the immoral thoughtlessness," as Bishop Butler called it—of my nominally Christian neighbours. Knowing little or nothing of the tremendous encroachments which physical science has made on the fabric of theology, nothing of the steady sapping which the authority of " Revelation " has undergone at the hands of the Ewalds, the Renans, the Strausses, and other literary critics of the Bible, they go on quietly ignoring theology just as if they had satisfied themselves that it was all the critics and savants had declared it to be. The average man, admitting that he is not religious, will frankly say that that is his fault, not the fault of religion. And he seems quite content that it should be so. He is, in fact, on a lower moral plane than the devils were reported to be. It was said of old time that the devils believe and tremble. But the man of to-day believes, or professes to believe, and does *not* tremble! He has been commanded not to covet, steal, bear false witness, commit adultery, or work on the Sabbath ; yet all these commandments he coolly and persistently breaks, mainly because, economic reasons apart, he has been threatened and bribed, but has not been instructed and has not been persuaded. He has been enjoined what to do and what to avoid, but he either has not been told the reasons for these commands, or reasons obviously inadequate have been assigned.

Because of all this and much more, I claim that the morals of the Decalogue and the Sermon on the Mount can have no place in Socialist ethics, except in so far as they stand the test of reason and the experience of how they operate in the formation of conduct and character to-day. The time has fully arrived when a code of ethics should be formulated which shall apply to all the relations, habits, and practices of life, enjoining the " Thou shalt " and the " Thou shalt not " on purely human and secular grounds.

Secularism, according to G. J. Holyoake, was called into being mainly for this purpose ; but Secularism as a positive philosophy has yet to arrive. Every person who attends chiefly to the business of this world is a Secularist ; but while the non-professing Secularist is " worldly " from carelessness or force of habit, the Secularist proper is supposed to be worldly from a reasoned belief that this is the *only* world. And yet it is but the sober truth to say that the Secularist devotes more attention to the Christian religion, for iconoclastic purposes, than the professed believer does for his soul's salvation. The enthusiastic Secularist who makes a religion of his irreligion is really less of a Secularist than the ardent Christian who devotes little attention to matters of belief, but busies himself in good works. Up to this point Secularism stands as a mere criticism of Bible religion. The arguments of the Secularist are mostly true, and his shafts of ridicule hit the mark ; which would, indeed, be difficult to miss, but to prove that the geology and astronomy of the Book of Genesis leave something to be desired, that the story of the Flood is open to question, or that the alleged slaying, by Samson, of so many Philistines with a very inadequate weapon is a narrative whose acceptance is attended by grave circumstantial difficulties—to prove all that is not particularly uplifting or even interesting. The exhibition of our neighbours' errors, either in belief or in conduct, may indeed prevent us from repeating their mistakes, but it will not prevent us from making equally egregious mistakes of our own. To show that the patriarchs were no better than they should have been will not of itself make us better than we are. In fact, the frequent dwelling on the follies and vices of others may, by lowering our estimate of character in general, have a tendency to reconcile us to an inferior standard of conduct and character for ourselves.

While the subject of morals has been rather neglected in Socialist philosophy, too much attention has been paid to it by the philosophers of every other school. The Christian Church has placed all the emphasis on personal " holiness " of a narrow, mechanical type, and has mostly neglected those social conditions which have so much to do with the character of a people. Supernaturalists have said to the people, " Be ye perfect," on the assumption, apparently, that by sheer force of will men could rise superior to the influences of heredity and environment alike. To the rich man, tempted by his idleness, his affluence, and the *ennui* of a life in which he can enjoy without producing, consume without creating, the command is given, " Be ye perfect ! " And after nineteen centuries of exhortation the answer is given, from time to time, in "The Maiden Tribute of Modern Babylon," the recreations of the Pelican Club, the Panama and Liberator frauds, the Cleveland Street and the Wilde and Russell scandals. To the proletarian, also, the counsel of perfection was held up— the proletarian, with his den in a mean and lowering back street, his daily drudgery, his cag-mag food, his shabby clothing, his bullying boss, his drinking, swearing, foul-mouthed mates, his worn wife and swarm of children, his hopeless future—to him or at him the Gospel has been preached ; in churches and mission halls, at charity dinners, from teetotal platforms, in tracts, in newspapers, and at street corners.

And if you would have *his* answer, do not expect it in words, but look for it at the football match, in the public house, in the Drink Bill and the Police Register.

The Supernaturalists are not the only moralists who have made this mistake. The Positivists and Agnostics also look for a complete moralisation of the individual before societary conditions can be set right. Herbert Spencer has put himself to some trouble to prove—what is, after all, but one side of the truth— that the character of the social unit determines the character of the social aggregate. Of course, it is not difficult to establish this partial truth ; and the wonder is that some of us should occasionally be found taking an apparently different view. The difficulty of carrying social progress very far without a certain amount of intellectual and moral progress having pre- ceded it, is well worth showing.

Suppose, for example, we were to adopt the heroic advice of a well-known Anarchist, and, carrying the torch to the slums, lead the people to the mansions, as he on one occasion put it. What would be the result ? We should certainly destroy one set of slums ; but is it not extremely likely that in a short time the mansions would become another set of slums ? It may be one of the injustices society has done to the slummite that it has rendered him in- capable of wisely using the wealth he has created, even if he were to get it ; but it is at least as well that we should recognise the fact while warring against its causes.

Again, there was a time when miners received

wages that for workmen were exceptionally high ; and
the results were that many of the men, unaccustomed
to prosperity, did not know how to use it and enjoy it
when it came. Some there were who, fearing the good
times might not last, put by money, and—whatever
may be said regarding the general utility of saving—
have most likely been the better for it during recent
distressful years. But the rest drank and gambled ;
they kept their fighting dogs and their fighting cocks ;
they dressed their wives in ridiculous finery ; they
bought pianos which no one in the house could play ;
and in many ways furnished the opponents of Socialism
with a stock of arguments which we have to dispose
of again and again in the course of propaganda, much
to our soul's weariness.

To give one more example, I need only point to the
manner in which the great body of the workers use
the occasional holidays they get at present to show
that a large amount of intellectual and moral progress
is required to make Socialism thoroughly workable
and satisfactory in its results.

The Socialist is, of course, ready with many forcible
answers to all these objections ; and it is because I
believe in the reasonableness of the possible answers
that I am a Socialist. He may point out, for instance,
that two wrongs do not make a right, and the fact
that the workers misspend some of their time and
money is no reason why they should be made to work
long hours for low wages. He may urge that if you
work men like brutes and deprive them of educational
opportunities, it is only natural that their pleasures
should be brutal. To the advice of the individualistic

moralist, whose counsel may be summed up in the words, " Man, mind thyself," he may retort that man has been minding himself, in a purblind sort of way, and neglecting societary conditions, too long. In all which the Socialist has certainly right and reason on his side. But these objections, and others such as these, have not been adequately met—have not been met often enough nor with sufficient clearness or completeness. Neither has our own view of morals been enough in evidence. It seems to me we are not as strong on conduct and character as we ought to be. The Jesus-Christ-and-him-crucified view of morals (and religion) has been so much before us that, in our natural nausea at its selfish and impossible scheme of personal " salvation," we show a tendency to run to the other extreme, overdoing the social and economic aspect of Socialism and overlooking the ethical and personal aspect of it.

In passing to and fro among Socialists, and in reading Socialist and labour journals, one is sometimes startled to find how negative are the ideas of many members of the party. They seem to be Socialists, not so much because Socialism will give them any positive thing to enjoy, but rather because it promises to relieve them of something they find it difficult to endure. Their motives are not constructive, but destructive. They are in the ranks, not because of the things they love, but because of the things they hate. While the prominent men in the movement prefer to speak of literature, art, science, travel, religion, better housing, more leisure, and physical and mental development, the average member of a

Socialist organisation finds his interest chiefly in the sins of his pastors and masters ; and bitter grumbling and blatant, clumsy denunciation of the present are more frequently to be heard from him than hopeful speculative discussion as to the future. A banal diatribe fetches his applause much more readily than the calm and lucid statement of a striking and com- prehensive general proposition. Then, again, how often do we hear science and art pooh-poohed by Socialists as matters without interest to men and women at the present day ? I feel inclined to ask these negationists, " What do *you* want Socialism for ? " Is it not in order that we may have oppor- tunities of studying the things of nature and art, learning some of the discoveries of scientists, building up for ourselves a well-equipped and fully-developed mind and body ? While some of us are disposed to look upon Socialism as that which must be realised before we can *begin* to live, there are others who behave as if their interest in life would have ceased were there no objects left upon which to pour out the vials of their wrath and scorn.

But, it may be asked, What has all this to do with morals ? To say that the average Socialist is not constructive, is not a man of mind, may imply intel- lectual defects ; but since very clever men have fre- quently been very great rogues, mental limitations cannot have much to do with morality. This opinion, very generally held, is to my mind disproved by criminal statistics, which show a decrease of crime with the improvement of education and the development

of habits of reading.*   The " educated " criminal may
be a " smart " man ; but I have never met with a
person of real culture who was addicted to sharp or
shady practices. I do not say there are no rogues
among the men of culture. The fact that a Bacon or
a Poe gets found out once in a century indicates that
there are others such who merely escape the infamy
following detection because they are not detected. But
so far as the present writer's reading and experience
enable him to judge, such cases are gratifyingly
exceptional. The superficial smartness of the flashy
blackguard never, to a person of fair discrimination,
covers the radical crookedness, vulgarity, and shallow-
ness of his nature. A defective theory of causation is
perhaps the chief characteristic of the vicious ; and
surely education does much to develop in men the
power of estimating the consequences of vicious acts
—to say nothing of the fact that education breeds men

* I have been accustomed to regard this as generally known
to persons of intelligence. But a well-known Socialist lecturer
having recently taken exception to my statement on this head, it
occurs to me that the figures may be given with advantage.

CRIME IN ENGLAND AND WALES IN THE YEARS NAMED.

Year.		Population.		Convictions.
1841	...	15,929,492	...	27,760
1851	...	17,982,849	...	27,960
1861	...	20,119,344	...	18,326
1871	...	22,712,266	...	16,269
1881	...	29,974,439	...	11,353

NOTE.—The first three sets of figures are from Hoyle's
" Crime in England and Wales " (1875), pp. 37-60 ; the last two
sets from the *Financial Reform Almanack*, " Statistics of Crime "
and " Census Returns."

of better social instincts, men who do not require
penalties to deter them from committing embezzlement
or murder. Inasmuch, therefore, as the acquisition
of knowledge and the development of the reasoning
powers tend to the improvement of the whole
character, intellectual culture is inseparably bound up
with ethical culture—is, in fact, a large part of ethical
culture itself.

I want us, then, to be stronger on the personal
virtues, such as Diligence, Courage, Truthfulness,
Public-Spiritedness, Honesty, Charity, Chastity. We
are mostly prepared, I think, to admit that the organisation of society upon a Social-Democratic basis could
not produce its proper fruits without a much higher
average moral and intellectual standard than exists in
any civilised community to-day. And since, as Oliver
Wendell Holmes has said, " In order to reform a man
you must begin with his grandmother," it follows that
you have to begin to cultivate here and now the
virtues, the needs, and the tastes of the properly-
developed and civilised man. Indeed, I am of opinion
that, until "the masses" urgently feel the need of
the life-conditions—the hearty human fellowship, the
leisure, travel, knowledge, and generous surroundings
—which Socialism would afford, we shall not have
Socialism. For, although I cannot see that the commercial system can last much longer in its present
form, still, without an intellectually and morally
awakened proletariat, there is no saying what societary
quagmires we might have to flounder through before
reaching " the cities of the Commune." Thus I have
rather a grudge against myself and the mass of my

fellow Socialists on the ground that we have neglected morals. The investigation of the workings of capitalistic society, and the work of proving that landlords and capitalists are leading a life of legalised brigandage—indispensable as that sort of study and propaganda may be—is not, to the propagandist, a high form of ethical culture.

CHAPTER II.

THE PARTICULAR AND THE GENERAL.

"The unfailing criterion in all such personal matters is—how do they affect our neighbours? If well, then we are doing right; if ill, then we are doing wrong."—ROBERT CHAMBERS.

A few years ago E. Belfort Bax made a characteristic-ally courageous and original effort to formulate a new and non-supernatural ethic. But the two papers* in which he propounds his views on ethics, admirable though they are, leave much to be done in the same department, as Bax would probably be the first to admit. Besides being general and abstract in character —especially "The New Ethic"—they are somewhat hard reading. Written in a scholastic style, they show a passion for scientific precision of statement which I should think frequently defeats the object the author has in view—namely, the plain one of making his meaning absolutely clear. These papers are also very negative; and the morals discussed in "Practical Ethics" are those of the present transition period, not those of the more fully-developed Social-Democratic State. In these papers Bax is critical rather than constructive; and although there is still much criticism

* "The New Ethic" (in *Ethics of Socialism*) and "A Socialist's Notes on Practical Ethics" (in *Outlooks from the New Standpoint*). Social Science Series. (London: Swan Sonnenschein and Co.)

to be done, I think it is to be regretted that in Socialist literature generally the chemist's "method of exhaustion" is so much in favour—our writers, like our speakers, preferring to exclude error rather than present the truth, to deny what they do not believe rather than to affirm what they do believe. A desire to avoid the appearance of preachiness may, perhaps, account for Bax's neglecting to apply the searching general principles laid down in " The New Ethic." But the applications require to be made all the same.

Bax gives an illustration of Socialist morality which, excellent though it be, only serves to prove and elucidate my contention that there is scarcely any positive ethical foundation for the men and women who are to enjoy the blessings of communal life in the years to come. Bax's illustration is the case of the Atheistical sergeant of the Commune, who, without hope of future reward, stands at his barricade awaiting certain death *"pour la solidarité de le genre humaine"* (" for the solidarity of the whole human race") as he says in answer to a question. It is impossible to study this example of unalloyed heroism without being moved to admiration of the type of character it displays, and profound gratification that the Service of Man can evoke feelings and conduct as lofty as ever the Service of God has done. It is, indeed, an ungrateful task to have to point out that there is something lacking here—that the illustration and the principle it embodies help us only a slight way in the direction of establishing a social ethic founded on purely secular considerations. For we cannot always be going to the barricades. Life does not consist

merely of fighting for *le genre humaine*. To no incon-
siderable extent it consists of minding one's own
business: and in studying social and secular ethics
what we want to know is not so much how to treat
our enemies *now* as how to live on terms of peace and
goodwill with our friends *then*.

Fortunately, however, Bax does lay down a really
lucid and comprehensive* principle to guide us in this
matter. This principle he expresses in two propositions, the one the correlative of the other: (1)
" Every act necessarily involving cruelty is *per se*
immoral; (2) no act not necessarily involving cruelty
is *per se* immoral." In " The New Ethic " as it origin-
ally appeared (in *The Commonweal*) this principle was
more conveniently and, as I think, more correctly
expressed in the canon that " for conduct to be justly
condemned under the New Ethic it must be proved
to be necessarily and directly anti-social." In " The
New Ethic " as republished, along with other essays,
in book form, this passage is omitted: but it is so
much more portable and convenient than the other dual
proposition that I shall take the liberty of retaining it
and using it here.

Bax's axiom, then, is that that act which is anti-
social is immoral, and, I would add, that only. This
is what Matthew Arnold would have described as
" altogether admirable "; but what we want now is
that some one should, in the light of this canon, tell
us a few of the hundred-and-one things that *are* anti-
social; and how and why they are so. It is the easiest
thing in the world to gain assent to general principles;

* In *Outlooks from the New Standpoint*, p. 111.

but when you come to apply those principles to concrete cases, most marked differences of opinion will be
discovered.

Of much of the current discussion of high ethics it
may fairly be said that it represents a somewhat
wasteful expenditure of literary effort. Writers such
as Guyau, Bixby, and ("in "The Data of Ethics,"
at any rate) Spencer insist on treating ethics in terms
of general principles, forgetting that the matters about
which we disagree are not general principles, but
rather what a given general principle involves in a
particular case. Life is made up of details, of habits
and practices, good and bad; and to discuss morals
otherwise than with reference to specific acts is to
beat the air. The sterility of abstract principles has
been emphasised again and again since the period of
the Renaissance. It is the burden of Bacon's refrain
in the "Novum Organum" and "The Advancement
of Learning." It received hard knocks at the hands
of Locke and Newton. The necessity for philosophy
being positive and concrete was the theme which,
above all others, inspired the pen of Auguste Comte;
and George Henry Lewes may well conclude his
"History of Philosophy" with the statement that
modern philosophy began with Bacon and a method
and ended with Comte and a method, the intervening
centuries being prolific of great names and voluminous
works, but very largely barren of practical con-
clusions. All this, however, does not prevent the
continued coining of formulas and the spinning of
cobwebs of generalisation. The investigations pursued
by Darwin among the coral islands, his observation of

the habits of earthworms, his experiments in the crossing of pigeons, and his attention, in exposition, to the minutest detail that might affect his theory, stand as a reproach to those who would seek to dismiss subjects so great and so complicated as are sociology and ethics with general propositions which may mean anything or nothing, according to the use made of them.

CHAPTER III.

HAS THE INDIVIDUAL A "RIGHT" TO HIMSELF ?—
WITH A DIGRESSION.

" It can easily be shown of all duties said to be owing to ourselves, that they are, more comprehensively, duties owing to society "—ROBERT CHAMBERS

BEFORE proceeding farther I wish to affirm the principle that a man has no absolute right to himself as against the community. He has no " right " to dispose of his energies in an anti-social manner, no right to take away his life. Society gave it him, and nourished and clothed and housed and educated him when he was unable to do these things for himself ; without the aid and service of his fellows he would probably be unable to live. In short, his obligations to society are such and so many that only a lifetime of his best effort is sufficient to repay the debt he owes. Anything, therefore, that tends to impair his usefulness to himself and to society, society has a right to brand as immoral because anti-social.

To say that the individual has no " right " to take away his own life may seem a somewhat off-hand treatment of a very debatable subject. It may be argued that, inasmuch as the individual is not consulted as to whether he wishes to be born or not, he ought to be left free to decide whether he shall retain the unsolicited, and in some instances doubtful, privilege of living. Now, with the very highest sense of the sacredness of life—a sense much higher, surely, than is possessed by those who, without protest, allow men, women, and children to be slowly murdered by insidious process of devitalisation in factory, field, and mine, in workshop and in slum dwelling (when not cut off by preventible slaughter and sudden death)— with, I say, the highest respect for human life, I think there is still room for something being said in favour of a form of "suicide." Putting aside the question of reward or punishment in a future state, of which we have no scientific evidence, I contend that a case can be made out for a species of mortal extinction which is not murder, which is not carried out for punitive purposes, and which is not exactly suicide either. In the case of one whose existence has become a prolonged bodily agony, whose cure has been despaired of by the most competent medical men, and who has no desire to live, I can see no reason why a merciful extinction, a scientifically-conducted euthanasia, should be denied, due provision being made for the dependants, if any. Look at this matter how I can, from the point of view of the new ethic, social and secular and humanitarian as that ethic is, there is nothing to be said *against* such a proposal. On the other hand, when we consider how much a person will hopelessly endure to-day before taking leave of life by self-inflicted death, and when we con- sider how unnecessarily cruel the suicide's death frequently is, there seems much to be said *for* the deliberate and socially-sanctioned euthanasia. It is

not for the moralist to say what the surgery of such
an operation should be; that is the business of the
medical expert ; though humanity prompts one to ask
why it is that communities which still retain the
barbarous and degrading institution of capital punishment have not thought of substituting ether or chloro-
form for the gallows and the electric current, with
which occasional ghastly experiments have been
made ?   A tribunal would require to be appointed for
the consideration of the presumably rare applications
for mortal extinction ; and such a tribunal would
require to have absolutely clear proof of the desire
for euthanasia on the part of the person in whose
name application was made ; while in order to ensure
against mere murder being carried out under the
sanction of the law, independent public officials would
require to be entrusted with this last duty. To persons
suffering from mental maladies caused by vital and
permanent injuries to the brain the same privilege
should be granted if sought for. But a too ready
compliance would in all cases be guarded against, on
the plain ground that " while there is life there is
hope." To persons afflicted with mere hypochondria,
euthanasia should be denied, inasmuch as mental
distress without a primary and vital physical cause
often proceeds from a morbid self-love which time
would, in many cases, cure. In the Social-Democratic State, with humane feeling at its maximum,
there would be less reason than ever to fear that
the practice of painless extinction would lead to a
diminished respect for life. And it is incredible that
the community of the future, with its ample resources,

should grudge the generous maintenance of the sick
and helpless. Socialism, however, is a philosophy of
life rather than of death. And although the normal
man is not always in the flush of health and high
spirits himself, he is rarely so miserable as to find a
discussion of the ethics of suicide an entertaining
topic. Having done what I believe to be my duty by
a gruesome theme in applied ethics, I gladly pass to
more cheerful considerations. I need hardly add that
no one save myself is responsible for the opinions here
set forth.

I must ask the reader who has followed me thus
far to return to the postulate (as academic gentlemen
would call it) with which we set out. It was, that
the individual has no absolute right to himself.

There is reason to doubt whether, in our view of
conduct, we always take into account the implications
of a principle so very comprehensive as this. If we
did, there would surely be less talk and less writing
about what are called " self-regarding acts."

It is frequently said of persons who are notably
careful in money matters that they have the self-
regarding virtues highly developed. In point of fact,
however, the man " of frugal mind " may be less self-
regarding than the person who spends lavishly. He
may have dependants, and his pecuniary caution may
be practised for their sake ; whereas the lavish person
may be prodigal of his means to the hurt of those
dependent upon him. The recklessly " generous "
person is usually parsimonious in some direction
or another. And apart from the fact that profuse
liberality has frequently a quite egotistical and vain-

glorious motive, it sometimes happens that one who has persisted in going his own heroic road, and running unnecessary risks of which his friends have vainly warned him, falls back upon those friends when the consequences of his folly recoil on him, and the time of need comes. It cannot be too strongly insisted that we are to-day, and always will be, so interdependent that the individual has no moral right to gaily rush into danger and difficulty on the plea that his acts are purely self-regarding and no concern of his neighbours.

It is the boast of many honest, impulsive souls in unpopular movements that they " speak their mind " ; that they " talk straight " ; that they " hew to the line, let the chips fall how they may." But is it not consistent with our experience that these well-meaning, headlong persons bring upon themselves a species of retribution whose consequences are not by any means wholly confined to themselves ? Who is there that has not within the circle of his acquaintance working men who have lost their employment through gratuitously attempting to ram unpalatable opinions down resentful throats ? Or business men who, neglecting their own affairs for those of the public, have landed themselves in the Bankruptcy Court, destroyed their usefulness to a great movement, and ended by blaming their principles for that which in reality was due to their own lack of ordinary prudence and judgment. The common weal will always require and will always command men and women who neither fear nor grudge the sacrifice of self in a worthy cause. But the moral man, recognising his obligations of service in many and diverse directions, will avoid quixotic immolation;

will, for the good of his cause, count the cost ere he
spends himself, remembering that a cheap martyrdom
may be to those who come after rather more of a
warning than an example. The liberty of the subject
can, beyond doubt, be carried much too far on the
ground that one's acts are purely self-regarding.

For myself, I confess I have a difficulty in determining what a purely self-regarding act may be. It
seems tolerably certain that such practices as drinking,
masturbation, the smoking or chewing of opium, even
the consumption of "infinite tobacco" (after the Tenny-
sonian manner)—all come under the ban of the Socialist
ethic, inasmuch as they detract from the social efficiency
of the individual as man or woman, father or mother,
citizen or wealth producer. It cannot be too strongly
insisted upon that the individual holds his powers of
mind and of body in trust for his fellows as well as for
himself ; and that the sanction of the new ethic cannot
be extended to acts which lead to the impairment of
faculties whose fullest and best exercise the community
requires from their possessors.

I can think of just one species of act that might
perhaps be viewed as self-regarding. At least, no
social and secular argument readily presents itself
against it. I refer to the act for which the brilliant
and wretched Wilde is to-day the associate of felons.
In view of the exclamations of bated horror over this
offence, and the tacit assumption that it stands second
only to murder in its enormity, it may be worth while
to point out that, tested by a non-theological ethic, it
is not quite certain that such practices are immoral at

all.* Revolting and " unnatural," but not necessarily anti-social on that ground. If it can be proved that sodomy involves physical injury, as is not unlikely, then the measure of the injury will be the measure of the immorality. But if not physically injurious, it is not easy to see under what category it could be condemned as immoral. Whatever the Marquis of Queensberry may think, the matter is primarily one for the medical man. Whether these practices are bad or indifferent, one is glad to think that they are physically so offensive to most men that that alone would suffice to prevent anything like their widespread prevalence. With the man who has no radical twist or lesion in his nature, it is enough that fire burns, that snakes bite, and that excrement stinks.

It is true the Legislature cannot deal prohibitively or punitively with every species of offence. It cannot well prevent people from drinking tannin instead of tea (as seemed to be desired by some of the Irish members in the last Parliament) ; it cannot check the development of neurotic tendencies in literary men by limiting their allowance of tobacco and compelling

* An Italian, writing to a popular London weekly, expressed surprise that Wilde's offence should be treated as a crime, and stated that it would not be so treated in his country. The reason why sodomy holds the place it does in the English Criminal Code appears to lie in the fact that Henry VIII., believing the practice to be not uncommon in monasteries, availed himself of it as one further means of vamping up charges against the monks whose property he wanted. One of the instructions given to the commissioners sent out to find pretexts for confiscating the monastery lands was to " see if the Abbott had any boyes lyeing with him."

them to take more outdoor exercise ; it cannot deal
with the secret sins of youths and maidens at public
schools ; nor can it compel all strong-minded women
to dress well and to remember that soap and water
are among the indispensable resources of civilisation.
With such matters the Legislature had better not try
to cope even if they represent habits and practices
that are *not* merely self-regarding.   Convenience and
expediency forbid universal State-interference with bad
habits.   But what the civil law cannot accomplish and
should not attempt may nevertheless be not unworthy
of the attention of the practical moralist.   It is the
business of the latter to compass by reason and ridicule
that which the law cannot secure by either the strength
of its arm or the length of its reach.

CHAPTER IV.

"THE CLEANLINESS OF THE SEXES."

"But you must know that we of these generations are strong and healthy of body and live easily ; we pass our lives in reasonable strife with nature, exercising not one side of ourselves only, but all sides, taking the keenest pleasure in all the life of the world. So it is a point of honour with us not to be self-centred ; not to suppose that the world must cease because one man is sorry ; therefore we should think it foolish, or if you will, criminal, to exaggerate these matters of sentiment and sensibility : we are no more inclined to eke out our sentimental sorrows than to cherish our bodily pains ; and we recognise that there are other pleasures besides love-making. You must remember also that we are long-lived, and therefore that beauty both in man and woman is not so fleeting as it was when we were burdened with self-inflicted diseases. So we shake off these griefs in a way which perhaps the sentimentalists of other times would think contemptible and unheroic, but which we think necessary and manlike. As on the other hand, therefore, we have ceased to be commercial in our love matters, so also have we ceased to be artificially foolish."—WILLIAM MORRIS.

THERE is no Socialist marriage, nor is there, so far as I am aware, any specifically Socialist theory as to sexual morality. But the definite change in economic arrangements which Socialism involves will naturally carry with it certain changes in other aspects of life which we may forecast without entering the domain of prophecy ; and it is not remarkable that, among Socialists who understand the import and most probable consequences of the economic change, there should

be a large measure of unanimity on sex questions.   In
common with all who have studied the ethics of sex
from the standpoint of social requirements and without
reference to theological dogma, the Social-Democrats
are heretical on the relationship of the sexes.   The
institution of marriage as it exists to-day is open to
criticism in so many of its essential features, and it
has, in fact, been so frequently attacked and so ineptly
defended, that anything like a detailed restatement of
the case against it would be a departure from the
purpose of these chapters.   After the judicial marshal-
ling by Mill of the arguments against the subjection
of women ; * the solid and exhaustive work of Bebel,
and the light skirmishing done by Mrs. Caird ; after
" Tess " and " The Woman Who Did," and now
latterly " Jude the Obscure," one has no heart to
flaunt the flag of negation more than is absolutely
necessary.   What I think we are now feeling the
need of is some more or less positive statement of the
ethics of sex relations as they are likely to stand in
the future rather than their past history or present
position.   And yet I suppose a certain brief recapitu-
lation of the arguments against the existing property
marriage is inevitable.

Apart, then, from the fact that women frequently
enter upon the married state as a means of escape
from the special exploitation to which female labour
is in most branches subject, we consider that the
marriage bond, after it has been consummated, is
much too hard and fast.   We believe in marriage for
better or worse only so long as both of the contracting

* See Appendix B at end.

parties are satisfied with their lot. We hold that incompatibility of temperament ought to be considered sufficient ground for divorce, due provision being, of course, made for the children. We contend, with Fichte, that affection alone makes and sanctions the union; that without that the married state is simply one of lifelong prostitution; that the society woman of 25 who to-day marries a hoary old sinner of 70 differs from the woman of the street only in that the consequences of her sin are not so disastrous to her. But to believe in the facilitation of divorce; to hold that the child born of affection, whether it be born in wedlock or not, is in the true sense a " natural " child, which ought to have equal rights with children born in wedlock; to hold that a woman is not necessarily morally " ruined," as the cant phrase goes, because, although not legally married, she has borne a child sound in mind and body into the world ; to believe in the wholesomeness of a freer sexual relation in general is a very different thing from believing in promiscuous intercourse of the sexes. If affection be the sanction of the sexual act, it is clear that no sentiment worthy of that name could be transferred suddenly and frequently from one person to another. We see that even under the existing system men and women who live together in the relation of " concubinage " adhere to one another as faithfully as though they had been married by all the Bishops in the House of Lords. In spite of frequent quarrels and temporary separations, they almost invariably come together again—a circumstance all the more significant when we take into account the general moral looseness of those who, as

things are, live in this relationship. That a couple,
with few of those ties of mutual respect and community of domestic and parental interests which bind
the average legally married couple together, should
continue faithful to one another throughout the greater
part of a lifetime is surely a striking tribute to the
strength of the monogamic instinct.

But, it may be roundly asked, Is chastity a virtue,
and is there such a vice as unchastity ? For one of
the answers we may turn to Bax, whose statement of
the position, whether we agree with it or not, has the
merit of clearness. He lays down the proposition that
the sexual act is *per se* neither good nor bad, but indifferent. That is to say, he regards it as a bodily
function, which, in itself indifferent, might be rendered
immoral by the attendant circumstances, as, for instance, if a friend's wife were treacherously seduced.
(He would probably allow us to add that excessive
sexual indulgence is immoral because of its bodily
consequences.) I find it impossible to agree with this
view, which leaves the element of physical modesty
out of account. Indeed, Bax himself says, later on in
the same paper,* that " prostitution for private gain is
morally repellent," while a reference he makes to "the
mystical theory of the sex relation " shows that he is
aware it is not usual to regard the sexual act merely
as a bodily function. If sexual intercourse were
merely a physical function, like eating and drinking,
there would be no moral reason why it should not be
publicly consummated, as it is among primitive peoples
like the Esquimaux, the South Sea Islanders, and the

* " Outlooks from the New Standpoint," pp. 115 and 124.

Maoris.* Now, whether this would be right or wrong, it is certainly what the most thoroughgoing "free lover" would not care to see becoming general.

The sexual act is one of those physical functions of which civilised man is instinctively ashamed, and it is natural and desirable, were it only in the interests of pleasure, that it should be privily consummated In a civilised community, with non-sexual intimacy between the sexes in business, pleasure, and social intercourse, a sexual ethic is necessary were it only to keep sex considerations as much as possible in the background. *Contretemps* arising from sex are sufficiently numerous and awkward in social life already ; but to abolish the distinction between married and single, and to transform all between the ages of 15 and 50 into "eligibles" —into possible cohabiters—would be found socially intolerable. It is well known that the relations of unmarried women with married men are much more frank and unembarrassed than with single men—for the obvious reason that the position of the former is so far settled that cap-setting motives are out of the question. As regards the possibility of a genuine friendship and nothing more between the sexes, Plato is a bit of a humbug ; but if a Platonic friendship be possible at all between the sexes it is possible between what the football players called married and single.

While it cannot be said that the sexual act is in itself immoral (which would appear to be the ancient Jewish and modern Christian view), irregular, that is, promiscuous—sexual indulgence is fairly open to the condemnation of the social ethic. Physical modesty

* Reclus, Letourneau.

is a flower of civilisation whose bloom cannot be preserved side by side with the rank growth of promiscuity. The promiscuous is the unchaste; the connection consecrated by sex love and deliberate choice, by physical and spiritual affinity, is the chaste union. The anti-social feature of unchastity is not merely or chiefly, in married persons, the wound inflicted on the husband or wife who realises that his or her partner has been unfaithful,* that their common joys and sorrows, their common hopes and fears, have not availed to make them as one flesh till death does them part; that a gulf yawns between them; that they are as strangers living together in a relationship out of which the spirit of unity and delicacy has gone. It is not, I say, merely or chiefly on this ground that unchastity would be condemned in the coming time, but because of the havoc it works on the individual, whether married or single, who gives way to irregular promptings. Experience shows that the sexual appetite if gratified in forbidden directions, grows abnormally, and leads men and women alike into the grossest and most grovelling prostration of intellect and the most humiliating positions. Despite the marital customs of the East, there is in the average human animal a strong monogamous instinct; and it seems tolerably certain that promiscuous sexual connections would always be condemned by public opinion. Not merely the public opinion of Mr. Paterfamilias Fogey and his married sister Mrs. Grundy, but the healthy public opinion which believes in physical modesty and

---

* Though this would be a case where Bax's axiom as to cruelty would come in.

the fidelity of partners in a solemn contract, and which despises the man who prowls around at night like a tom cat, his one absorbing passion the desire for gratification of a physical impulse. The men and women of the future, having their intellectual natures more highly developed than the robbed and toilworn drudges of to-day, will, in spite of greater sexual freedom, be less rather than more sensual, just as the least refined men and women of the nineteenth century are superior to those early Irish kings who are said to have copulated with their wives in presence of the assembled court. And so the young unmated men and women of coming years will find themselves surrounded by a public sentiment more severe against breaches of the sexual law than ever.

For the rest, it may be said that the more socialised we become the more we shall recognise that anything that causes a man or woman to practice concealment from husband or wife, father or mother, sisters or brothers, is an anti-social thing because it divides us from one another and engenders the vice of hypocrisy. As the evolutionists have so well shown, all the appetites have been given to us in excess. The genital organs, in common with most others, acquire with abnormal use the power, up to a certain point, of abnormal secretion ; but the other powers of the body suffer in proportion to this abnormal development, and the suffering and deterioration are not confined to the individual himself, but extend to his children and his children's children. Who can forget the terrible scene in Ibsen's " Ghosts " where Oswald Alving, the son of a dead rake, and himself on the

D

verge of insanity, tells his mother that a great Parisian doctor has declared that he (Alving) has been "worm-eaten from his birth" as a consequence of his father's excesses ?

The gratification, in illicit directions, of the sexual appetite appears to grow to such an extent on the person who has given way to it, creating a morbid desire for fresh " conquests " and variety of victims, that it distracts men from the solid and enduring pleasures and utilities of life. Libertinism has, more-over, a coarsening effect on the general character of the licentious person ; and even if it were not repug-nant to the acquired taste of many men and most women, it would stand condemned as anti-social on that ground alone. In the society of the future mental and moral coarseness will be reckoned a much more objectionable characteristic than it is in our present life of social storm and stress, where the strong man, the man who can make and take and command, is the admired man. With the need for Nelsons and Gambettas no longer existing to the same extent as now, men will be judged more by their static than by their dynamic qualities. The Social-Democratic State is not going to produce a race of domesticated creatures who are mere " nice men for a tea party," but neither will it produce men whose vices are only forgiven them on account of their capacity.

With the safeguards of affection between husband and wife and " independence " on the part of women, both married and single, sexual promiscuity and the tyranny of man, the present economic master and sultan of the bedchamber, cannot fail to be reduced to a minimum even if physically and mentally he should in most cases be the stronger.

I avoid the use of the phrase economic equality, because absolute economic equality between the sexes is impossible. There are physical causes that will always incapacitate women from entering the field at will as public servants of the Social-Democratic State. For a few days of every month women require rest, although to-day the women of the industrial class seldom get it. Again, during the child-bearing period women are economically incapacitated. To render women " independent " of their male relatives at such a time, some scheme for the endowment of mothers by the community would be necessary ; and inasmuch as in the society of the future every normal child born would be regarded as a possible and probable mental, moral, and economical gain to the State, maternity would surely have such honour paid to it as never before. Instead of grudgingly and mistakenly viewing each fresh-comer into the world as a mouth to be fed and a back to be clothed—which is the Neo-Malthusian view—it would be regarded as the possessor of mental and physical faculties enabling it in the normal con-ditions of a well-ordered commonwealth to give more than it would take, to produce or create more than it would consume or destroy.

The Social-Democratic State is not likely to insist, as the State does to-day, on particular forms of marriage. But in all probability marriage will always be entered upon with more or less of ceremony. It is right that the parties to a covenant so serious and important should be made aware of the significance of

the step they are taking ; and this end would always
be in some measure assisted by the making of definite
promises in presence of witnesses. Again, without
having any special fondness for ecclesiastical formalism
and tutelage, I still think that the sound advice sometimes given by the sacerdotal fugleman at a wedding
would not be entirely omitted in the secular marriages
of the future. I see no reason why we should not
straightway begin to have Socialist marriages in our
branch organisations. While we may cordially detest
many phases of the Little Bethel spirit, the church
feeling would still appear to be a natural and perhaps
permanent factor in human nature. By " church
feeling " I mean the instinct which prompts men and
women holding certain beliefs to come together in a
public and social way, and give expression of, and
adhesion to, the beliefs they hold in common. It is
too much to expect that there will not be sects in the
Social-Democratic State ; and I see no reason why
the marriages of the future should not be solemnised
in the company of the faithful, whatever the nature of
the "faith" may be—one or more of the most eloquent
and impressive of the company of kindred souls
officiating. I trust that with parsonic readers these
expressions of opinion will be accounted unto me for
righteousness.

And now I want to say that I think a good deal too
much attention of the merely vague and shrieking kind
has been devoted to the sex question. The impression
has been created in some quarters that in the Socialist
movement every husband is looking wistfully past his
wife to other women, and that not a few of the wives

are looking past their husbands. This impression has been largely created by writers who are outside the movement rather than in it. There are so many noble and useful and absorbing interests in life apart from the gratification of the sexual feelings that even those who are not at ease in the bonds of matrimony experience no great difficulty in putting up with something less than idyllic conjugal felicity. While treasuring up what of genuine poetry and sentiment there are in his every-day life, the active man has no belief in the romantic notion, largely created by writers of fiction, that there is for every man and woman somewhere in the wide world some one being who is his or her physical and psychological affinity. Every day we meet people with whom we are satisfied we could jog along comfortably in the matrimonial harness. Married folk know that there are a hundred and one things in which a husband and wife—especially where there are children—enjoy a happy chumship, even where some of the deeper needs of their nature are not quite satisfied. Granted the facilitation of divorce, the equalisation of economic and political status as between men and women, with the endowment of mothers, and, as a mere matter of discussion and propaganda, there is not much of the sex question left. When one remembers this it is not always easy to subdue a feeling of anger when at public meetings, whatever the subject of discussion may be, some professed Socialist, who, we know, has not attended a meeting for perhaps three months before, and takes no part in the hard work of ordinary propaganda, rises to ask if the lecturer is in favour of Free Love!

The really earnest propagandist, recognising that the property marriage of to-day is very largely a necessity of the property institutions of to-day, will, without concealing his opinions on sex questions, devote his energy mainly to the fundamental work of helping on the economic change, and he will be careful to fall in more or less with the existing social requirements on matters of, to him, comparative indifference.

As Socialists we are not at present called upon to make a stand for everything that is right and proper and good and true and pure. There is some virtue in submitting to a partial and temporary self-effacement for the good of the cause ; but, to assert principles under circumstances which will injure our cause, injure ourselves, and for the time being damn the principles as well—that is mere " cussedness."

CHAPTER V.

THE ORIGIN OF ETHICS.

" We have now seen that actions are regarded by savages, and were probably so regarded by primæval man, as good or bad solely as they obviously affect the welfare of the tribe, not that of the species nor that of an individual member of the tribe. This conclusion agrees well with the belief that the so-called moral sense is aboriginally derived from the social instincts, for both relate at first exclusively to the community."—DARWIN.

To argue that ethics derive their existence from religion —which is the Theistic and popular view—is to transpose their relative positions, is, in the phraseology of the street, to put the cart before the horse. Ethical conceptions are a purely social and secular product. As social relations become more complex, new moral rules necessarily arise to cover the new contingencies. And with this growing complexity of social relations and formation of fresh ethical principles there comes an improvement in the religious conceptions of the people.

Thus we have the seed of Abraham starting on their career as a people with the gross god Jahveh, who is reported to be fond of the savour of roast kid, who is represented as enjoying the dripping of fat and blood from the sacrificial victims, and who early in the day is made to disapprove of the vegetarian offering of Cain and to prefer the bloody tribute of Abel. We

have him exhorting the tribes of Israel to the slaughter
of conquered peoples, the ravishing of their young
women, and the plunder of their goods and chattels—
the message being conveyed with a frankness not to
be outdone by the most shameless jingo of modern
times. In the earlier part of the Old Testament Jahveh
and his people recognise other gods, both explicitly and
implicitly, but as time wears on we find these early
polytheistic notions giving way to the idea that Jahveh
is the only God. The Jewish tribal god was simply
a glorified edition of the most typical Jew of the
period. Instead of God creating man in his own
image, it is man who has created his gods very faithfully in *his* own image. So that the jest in which
Colonel Ingersoll paraphrases Pope's saying—" An
honest man's the noblest work of God "—by declaring
that " An honest God's the noblest work of man," is
not a mere unmeaning travesty uttered for the sake
of the antithesis.

As a matter of history, we everywhere find the im-
provements in the conception of God and religion and
morality coming, not from the religious caste, but from
the lay-" prophet," whose mission throughout history
has been to advance morality in the face of the most
determined opposition of the priestly class. That
the priesthood has persecuted the philosophers, the
scientists, and the social reformers, and used religion
to justify and defend many horribly wicked and many
absurdly foolish things, is a commonplace ; but that,
unlike a large number of commonplaces, it has the
merit of being true, is amply shown by the terrible

catena of charges gathered together by Dr. Draper in his "Conflict of Religion and Science."

In the primitive community there would appear to be no ethic against theft, because, with the practical communism of such a society, there would be little motive or purpose for personal appropriation within the community, whereas theft from a neighbouring tribe would naturally be regarded as a virtue, as would also be the murder of enemies. In like manner the exogamic instinct which prompted the primitive man to seek a wife outside his own community would be held to sanction the capture and rape of women not belonging to the tribe. But with the increase of population, the growth of the arts, and the subdivision of labour and property, offences against property would creep in. As theft within the community began to be practised, the victims of spoliation would gradually compare notes, a public opinion would be developed, and eventually theft would be condemned by the priest and punished by the authorities. With the development of commerce between communities, the necessity of maintaining friendly relations with outsiders would lead to the general condemnation of acts likely to disturb those relations. But the initiative in these moral movements would not naturally come from religion, whose authorised exponents, always a privileged class, would be largely removed from the ordinary concerns of social life, and who, moreover, offered up human sacrifices on their altars and kept prostitutes in their temples long after murder and fornication had been condemned by non-theological ethics. Moral and social changes would largely emanate from obscure and comparatively poor men—the Virginiuses, Wat Tylers, and Massaniellos of their time—whose helplessness would render them the most easy and likely victims of anti-social acts. It is from the common people and the relations of everyday life that we trace the growth of morality. The individual, resenting the anti-social act by whieh he is the sufferer, soon meets with others who are smarting under a similar feeling; they start an agitation and a log-rolling; and whether the acts of which they make common complaint are to be the subject of statute law or not, will depend on the nature of the acts themselves, the strength of the feeling against them, and the possibility of dealing with them by legal methods. If they are capable of being repressed by legal punishment they will be treated punitively; but if they are offences which it is neither possible nor desirable to treat as crimes, their condemnation will be left to the moralist, and their punishment to their own inseparable natural conse-quences, including the influence of public opinion.

The universally-known Golden Rule would at first take a negative form. Instead of exhorting to the positive practice of virtue (" All things, therefore, whatsoever ye would that men should do unto you, even so do ye also unto them "), it would simply warn off from evil (" Whatsoever ye would *not* that men should do unto you, even so do ye *not* also unto them "). The anti-social act would be branded as immoral before its obverse would be recognised as moral.

The Ten Commandments, although given forth by Moses in the name of religion, really arose out of the

recognition of certain acts that required to be dis-
couraged on social grounds and certain other acts
which on similar grounds required to be encouraged.
The Decalogue—like all "sacred" writings—had its
origin, and its several social and non-theological
commands were recognised, long before Moses produced the law in a codified form.⁰ Does anyone
maintain that stealing (except from the Egyptians),
or murder (except of enemies in war), or fornication
(except with the women taken captive in invasions of
hostile territory)—does anyone maintain that these
offences were not condemned before Moses forbade
them in the name of religion ? On the contrary, had
the moral sense of the Jewish people not already condemned these things as anti-social, they would not
have been prepared to accept the Mosaic condemnation of them as irreligious.

Morals being thus social and secular in their origin,
what we have to do on behalf of the ethics of the
Social-Democratic State is to separate them from
precepts enjoining duty to God and from any other
commands for which there is no social and secular
warrant. The former it is our business to justify,

* I am well aware that, as Jules Soury says (" The Religion of
Israel," p. 19) : " The grand and living picture which we admire
in Exodus and in Numbers has no historical likeness. We cannot
prove that a single law of the Decalogue goes back to Moses ;
on the contrary, we can prove that the greater number of the
laws have not this origin, especially with the additions which
accompany the two slightly differing versions of Exodus and
Deuteronomy." I am well aware of this, I say ; but I accept
Moses and make the most of him, as I accept Jupiter, Rip Van
Winkle, or any other attractive myth.

extend, and emphasise ; the latter we repudiate as ethical *impedimenta*, intellectual lumber in a store-house where all the room is wanted for furniture that serves a purpose.

CHAPTER VI.

CHARITY.

Charity suffereth long and is kind ; charity envieth not ; chari.y vaunteth not itself, is not puffed up, doth not behave itself unseemly, seeketh not its own, is not provoked, taketh not account of evil ; rejoiceth not in unrighteousness, but rejoiceth with the truth ; beareth [or covereth] all things, believeth all things, hopeth all things, endureth all things."—PAUL.

IN the revised version of the New Testament the word " charity " in the above passage has throughout given place to the word " love." This may be a more correct rendering ; but I prefer the term used in the authorised version. It is inevitable that words which in the earlier stages of a language have several meanings should at length be limited to a single meaning. In the interests of precision this is necessary and desirable. But those who would narrow the signification of the word " charity " to almsgiving are surely actuated by something other than a desire for precision. Is there not reason to believe that a commercial society, with its tendency to regard cash payment (inadequate even at that) as the one thing needful, has come to believe that the giving of doles to the poor is a sufficient expression of, or substitute for, the fine fraternal feeling spoken of by Paul—the charity which " suffereth long and is kind," which " is not puffed up," and which rejoiceth not in the unrighteousness of others as affording an excuse for its own injustice. It would be easy to characterise this as an uncharitable opinion ; but is it not certain that society *is* satisfied to express its spirit of charity through almsgiving ; nay, does not society grudge even the alms ?

With charity in the almsgiving sense there is no need to deal here. In the society of the future charity will mean only what it means in the First Epistle to the Corinthians—namely, the opposite of cynicism, the recognition of the good in our neighbours, and the accounting for, and excusing of, their defects, their foibles, and even their vices. But the spirit that " hopeth all things," that gives the benefit of the doubt, that explains and excuses where doubt there is none, does not require that we should *justify* foibles and vices. It is one thing to extenuate " defects of will and taints of blood " and a quite different thing to encourage and confirm the backslider in his pre- ventible lapses. Charity requires us, in the words of Walt Whitman, to " stand up for the stupid and the crazy " when angrily attacked with indiscriminate and purposeless invective ; but that does not mean that we are to condone evil acts and propensities that can be checked by exposure, denunciation, and exhorta- tions to better ways. Charity requires that we should approach the exposure of error or the assailing of vice, not with gleeful malignity or triumphant scorn, but with judgment and good intent.

The teaching of Socialism is already doing much to increase the spirit of charity. By its insistence on the potential equality of all men ; by pointing out that the physical or mental superiority of one class over another is in the long run entirely a matter of training, education, opportunity; by its upholding the claims of the hand and brain against the power of wealth and privilege, Socialism brings us face to face with the essential facts of manhood, and shows us how much poor and rich, dull and clever, oppressed and favoured have in common. The Socialist does not say that one man is as " good " as another ; but he does say that one man *might* have been as "good" as another, given a different set of opportunities. Socialism leaves to the empty Radicalism of the mere political democrat such assertions as that one man is as good as another, that all men are naturally equal, and that " Jack's as good as his master." Were such statements true, Socialism would be deprived of a considerable part of its *raison d'être*. The complaint of the Socialist against individualism is that it renders physical and mental excellence impossible for the vast majority of the people. If the worker could be as wise and informed as the typical member of the British Association ; if he could be as strong and handsome and long-lived as the men who ride to hounds and shoot over the moors in the long autumn afternoons, while he is gasping and sweltering in sewers and chemical works ; if he could be as eloquent and refined and self-possessed as the Cabinet Minister who represents his division in Parlia-ment—he would not so strongly covet for his class the education, travel, leisure, the fine atmosphere and surroundings that almost make the rich a different order of beings from the poor.

But while this general difference exists and breeds its inevitable fruit of scorn and uncharitableness, the

intellectual distinctions at least are being considerably
effaced by the levelling influence of education ; and in
spite of the development of a class consciousness and a
class war, the combatants have perhaps more in common now than they ever had before. They read the
same books and newspapers. They attend the same
public entertainments (though they sit in different
parts of the house).   In Britain and America at any
rate their dress is the same. Their ideas on public and
personal questions are largely similar. Through their
trade unions and friendly societies working men have
shown that they possess administrative capacity ; and
now that, possessing political power also, they express
their class consciousness in demands for class legislation, their position and needs become ever better
known and considered. We have long left behind us
the time when the proletarian was addressed as
"churl."   We have even left behind the later period
when he was called "fellow." To-day it is no longer
customary for the rich man, outside the workshop, to
address the workman with oaths and contumely.

To understand our neighbour's position, and how he
came to be what he is, is to sympathise with him, and
to cease to blame him for being what he is and cannot
help being. Of this sympathy is the spirit of charity.
The class war exists, and will be waged with increasing
vigour and intelligence as time goes on. But, although
the engagements in this war may be hot enough while
they last, and follow ever closer one upon another,
there is no reason why the political antagonism should
become a social rancour. Already men and women
step down and out of their class to help the workers

in their avowed object of ending class privilege; and the number of those who sympathise is surely not limited to those who take the extrene step of declassing themselves.

Without going the length of saying that *all* strife is at bottom misunderstanding, it is clear that much of it is so; and with all that is most fascinating in literature on the side of the social revolution; with the life, the needs, and the aspirations of the workers becoming so well known, it is not too much to expect that uncharitableness as between classes will progressively diminish until the class distinctions themselves disappear.

The diffusion of the scientific temper as applied to the gauging of character weakens the tendency to blame and increases the desire to explain. And the scientific temper will be the temper of the coming man. Cultivating the faculty of estimating the personal worth of our neighbours, we shall more and more discern that in the normal man the good predominates. Whether or not our neighbour's qualities be those that find most favour in our eyes, as time goes on we shall be in less and less danger of forgetting that it takes all sorts of people to make a world, and that there is room and there is need for our neighbours as well as ourselves.

But it may be asked, on what ground is uncharitableness to be condemned as anti-social? Is not the school for scandal a diverting seminary? And what injury does a light and epigrammatic scarifying inflict on the absent one? What the ear does not hear the heart does not grieve.

Well, to begin with, is not the frequent indulgence in uncharitable tittle-tattle an enormous abridgment

E

of the opportunities of serious and serviceable converse.
If we participate in the antipathetic dissection of our
neighbour's character need we be surprised if our neighbours do the same by us in our absence? What the
ear does not hear the imagination can conceive, and
the more our conscience pricks us the more lively are
the workings of fancy when we see our acquaintance
standing apart and, as we suspect, measuring to us as
we have meted to others. Oh, the wreck of reputations
by evil-speaking in the habitations of the smooth-faced!
How can we pretend that the scandalmonger only
lightly touches the sores of his victims? When we
hear an acquaintance raked fore and aft by a male-
volent and lying tongue, and shortly see the slanderer
effusively greet the injured one, our confidence in the
whole human species suffers a shock the impression
of which no amount of self-sacrifice on the part of our
fellows and no kindness experienced at their hands
ever quite effaces. We can never know how much
we have suffered at the hands of the uncharitable.
Averted looks, frigid handshakes, confidence and friendship obstinately withheld—how much of all this may be
owing to the work of some unknown and unsuspected
defamer! If our own disposition and regard for the use
of our time do not place us above uncharitableness,
the voicing of it in scandal may at least be checked by
the remembrance that the more injustice we inflict the
more injustice we shall sustain.

It was a happy instinct that led Matthew Arnold to
select from "The History of David Copperfield" the
characters of Murdstone and Quinion as types of the
Englishmen of to-day. Murdstone, with his harsh,

metallic nature, his narrowness, his lack of ideas and imagination, the value he placed upon being " firm," and his insistence on having his own way—Murdstone stands for all time as the incarnation of the serious middle-class Saxon of to-day ; and his characteristic feature is lack of sympathy. The sporting Quinion is a still commoner English type. He is the man who is to be seen at cattle shows, in public houses, and on racecourses. He may be identified by his knicker-bocker suit of checked tweed, his heavy boots and ribbed stockings, his cap, his loud tie, loud watch-chain, and loud apoplectic voice. He is not complete without a red face, a cigar, and a self-contained manner. Not that Quinion contains himself. He expresses his opinions freely, with a certain good-natured dogmatism ; and his laugh is the essence of unintentional brutality. He is one of the last men from whom you would expect *intellectual* sympathy. A less unloveable character perhaps than Murdstone ; but think of a population divided roughly into Murdstones and Quinions, and then imagine how the people who differ from these worthies must fare at their hands. Murdstone, with his church and chapel, his regular hours, his firm domestic management, his conventional clothes, his conventional whiskers, his conventional ideas – how can he or the other put up with ideas that have no prospect of hard cash, or material comfort, or civic "honours" attached to them.

The man of the future will be as different as possible. Hard cash and keeping up appearances can no longer be motives and springs of conduct with him. From toadyism he will be saved in spite of himself. With a living easily got, and no anxiety for old age, he will dig and plant and tend his flowers and his bees, he will go among shepherds on the hillsides and out with fishermen on the sea; but above all he will read and think and dispute. He will be a gossip in the sense that Socrates and Cephalus were gossips. His chief interests will be intellectual interests; and he will no more turn from a "queer fish," with new-fangled notions, than Quinion would turn from a good dinner, or Murdstone from a jointured and willing widow. With no suspicion of ulterior motives behind the spoken word of the casual acquaintance, his antipathies will be towards positive ascertained evils, not towards persons or theories. With joy in the present and hope for the future, there will be comparatively little room in his great good nature for the gall of the backbiter.

But charity requires something more than the mere avoidance of evil-speaking. It requires the manifesta-tion by word and deed of the affection or admiration we cherish for our friends. Reading the warm and doubtless sincere speeches delivered over the dead body of a brave, quiet soldier of the Revolution* the other day, one could not help remembering how little expression was given in his lifetime to the cordial feelings we all entertained towards him. It is the way of the world to publish obituary notices, biographical sketches, and reviews of the work of men and women who scarce received one word of praise or recognition while such words might still have been of use to them in lightening the burden or shortening the road. This, I say, is the way of the world; but it is not a kindly

* This was written shortly after the funeral of Stepniak.

way, it is not a social way, and it is not the way to get
the best and most serviceable effort out of one another.
The biographical notices, the subscription for one's
widow, "the storied urn or animated bust" for a man
who was allowed to live in obscurity and die in neglect
—are they not a trifle late considered as the recognition
and reward of a noble life. Were we as slow to cen ure
as to praise, as swift to reward as to punish, as ready to
speak and write words of encouragement as to come
down with the sword and flame of a more or less
righteous indignation, what an infinitely pleasanter
world it would be, and how much less the need for
indulging in homiletics on the subject of charity!

The coming social order will further charity because
it will give the ape and tiger in man a chance of dying
out; and if it breeds men and women with better
bodies, better heads, and better hearts, we need expect
no more, since, as Cotter Morison says, "There is no
remedy for a bad heart and no substitute for a good
one."

CHAPTER VII.

CHEERFULNESS.

"Some men are remarkable for pleasantness in raillery, others for apologues and apposite, diverting stories. This is apt to be taken for the effect of pure nature, and that the rather because it is not got by rules ; and those who excel in either of them never purposely set themselves to the study of it as an art to be learnt. But yet it is true that at first some lucky hit, which took with somebody and gained him commendation, encouraged him to try again—inclined his thoughts and endeavours that way, till at last he insensibly got a facility in it, without perceiving how ; and that is wholly attributed to nature, which was much more the effect of use and practice. I do not deny that natural disposition may often give the first rise to it ; but that never carries a man far without use and exercise, and it is practice alone that brings the powers of the mind as well as those of the body to perfection. . . . . We see the ways of discourse and reasoning are very different, even concerning the same matter, at Court and in the University. And he that will go but from Westminster Hall to the Exchange will find a different genius and turn in their ways of talking ; and one cannot think that all whose lot fell in the city were born with different parts from those who were bred at the Universities or in Inns of Court."—LOCKE.

WHAT is a virtue ? I should call it a mode of mind which expresses itself in conduct tending to promote social wellbeing. That is to say, acts are to be described as virtuous or vicious according as their social results are respectively good or bad. Now, if character is to be judged solely by its average social outcome, it is clear that all pro-social attributes must be regarded as virtues, and all anti-social attributes as vices. To regard as virtuous a person possessed of natural good qualities is philosophically correct, and, as it happens, it is also in accordance with popular, everyday opinion. Ordinarily we like and respect a man of good social qualities without any reference to whether those qualities are mainly natural or largely self-acquired.

Yes, granted, it may be said ; but why affirm the obvious ? Because it is just precisely the obvious and its implications that we oftenest forget. There is a species of reasoning which occasionally leads us to draw distinctions between the qualities that are evolved by the individual himself and those that have been indigenous with him from his birth. When, for instance, we see a person whom we know to be hot tempered mastering his natural choler we feel that, for the moderation which is the outcome of self-restraint, he deserves more " credit " than is due to the man of easy good-nature, whose forbearance costs him no effort. Though the social results may be in both cases the same, we sometimes speak of the one character-result as a virtue and of the other as merely a quality. To the person who conquers a vice or a defect we give the credit due to him who has done battle and with-stood temptation ; whereas of the person who has no thorn in the flesh to contend with we say : "Ah, yes! he is a good fellow—there is not much harm in him ; " but while we value him for the social beneficence of his character, we feel that a distinction ought to be made between a given virtue in his case and a similar virtue in the case of the man of " storm and stress." There is, however, nothing very philosophical about this desire to distinguish. The difference is merely one of mental process. In the one case virtue is spontaneous and reliable, in the other there is a conflict of motives, complexity in the process of evolution, and less certainty as to the result that will finally be evolved. But the difference between the two mental processes is one of degree, not of kind. For the man who resists the temptation presented by a natural defect does so by means of some natural advantage for which he deserves no more credit than the constitutionally good-natured man deserves for his good nature. And so there is no need to draw distinctions between virtues and qualities. We are quite entitled to regard as virtuous all mental states, whether spontaneous or complex, that make for social wellbeing.

Cheerfulness, then, is a quality if you will, but a virtue certainly. Conscious struggle with the opposing vice (melancholy), the play of motives, the weighing of arguments for and against, and the final conquest and possession of the virtue—these are scarcely factors in the attainment of cheerfulness, which would appear mainly to "come by nature," as Dogberry said of reading and writing. And yet how highly social is the property of a sane and quiet cheerfulness ! Can any-one who has read the *Phædo* ever forget that scene— bright and vivid for us in the page of Plato after the lapse of two thousand years—in which the serene old pagan spends his last hours in sprightly converse with his friends, showing his interest in human affairs and his concern for others even in the act of taking the poisoned cup from his weeping jailer ? Contrast that picture with the scene in which Shakespeare depicts the querulous last hours of King John. Whilst Socrates, with complete disregard of self, is anxious to comfort his friends by the exercise of those colloquial graces of which he was such a master, the distempered king apparently cannot infuse enough of petulance into his language :—

> " And none of you will bid the winter come
> To thrust his icy fingers in my maw ;
> Nor let my kingdom's rivers take their course
> Through my burned bosom ; nor entreat the north
> To make his bleak winds kiss my parched lips
> And comfort me with cold—I do not ask you much ;
> I beg cold comfort ;— and you are so strait
> And so ungrateful you deny me that."

The man who is about to be judicially murdered causes his friends temporarily to forget his approaching fate in a discussion on the immortality of the soul ; whilst the bundle of vices and appetites that has already lived too long piles one peevish hyperbole above another in its efforts to make the bystanders miserable. Cheerfulness is the salt of human fellow-ship; but how many fellowships are savourless through the efforts of Sir Fretful Plagiary !

I am afraid that the melancholiacs are not to be made cheerful by direct preaching and teaching. A man may be shamed out of the rudeness of giving way to fits of despondency and irritability without effort to prevent them, but the chances are that you will succeed only in taming him into the dulness of the " well-bred " person, a characteristic as far removed from cheerfulness on the one hand as it is from ill-temper on the other. Cheerfulness is not merely the negation of ill temper. It is a positive quality—a state of the mind depending largely, perhaps mainly, on the state of the body and the fortunes of the individual. It would be difficult to lay down any law of cheerfulness, difficult to persuade a man that he ought to be cheerful where he feels he has reason to be despondent. If all about him are happy, and he not so, then there are circumstances in his case to account for his despondency; and it will usually be found either that he has neglected some of the laws of life or that he has been unfortunate in his parentage. " The slings and arrows of outrageous fortune " do not, as a rule, make men confirmed pessimists. Give the average man a run of very moderate luck, and even after half a lifetime of buffeting he will become hopeful and cheerful. Without saying that " hope springs *eternal* in the human breast," it would be safe to say that the individual hopes for himself long after his friends have ceased to hope for him.

With incurable disease or inherited melancholia society cannot do much. It can, however, so regulate the conditions of life that men in general will have less cause than now to be despondent by reason of external circumstances; and the melancholiacs, belonging, as they largely do, to the leisured classes, will have an opportunity of losing somewhat of their hypochrondria in work for their living. Enforced activity is a rare dispeller of evil humours.

But if cheerfulness be a mental state which is not to be directly compelled—not to be secured by precept, by persuasion or menace, by bribes or penalties—it can still be indirectly induced by alteration of the environment and by changed habits of life. One great cause of irritability is what the vendors of patent medicines describe as "nervous debility." Bodily inactivity, with close and solitary application to sedentary pursuits, begets a high-strung self-consciousness and a habit of introspection and general analysis of life which, combined with the dyspepsia due to vitiated air and a preposterous diet, go far to explain morbid tendencies. The obvious remedies here are open-air exercise, change of scene and occupation, and extended social intercourse.

The person whose life is full of physical activity, intellectual interest, and social communion has no inclination to ask and answer questions as to the purpose and value of life. He is so intensely absorbed in "the things immediate to be done" that cravings after the absolute touch him scarcely at all. I am not speaking here of the automatic people who—

> " ——see all sights from pole to pole,
> And glance and nod and bustle by,
> And never once possess their soul
> Before they die."

Few Socialists desire to see the fussy Philistine type multiplied. When I suggest activity as a promoter of cheerfulness, I do not mean the restricted, getting-and-spending activity of the ignorant and flatulent man of affairs, but the noble and varied activity, mental as well as physical, of open-minded manhood and citizenship.

Apart from the change which may be effected in the temper of the individual by altering his environment and putting him in good bodily case, cheerfulness can be assisted by a reform in our social conventions. In non-Latin countries we are apt to put too high a value on mere gravity of demeanour. We esteem the man of puckered brow, without considering whether the creases in his forehead owe their existence to much thought or to ill-temper. We are so accustomed to integrity being accompanied by severity of manner that we distrust the man of pleasant address, and suspect sinister motives in the person who pays us compliments. The politeness of the French and Italians we despise, regarding it as a badge of moral and perhaps mental inferiority, fit only for barbers and waiters.

So deep-seated with us is the tradition of solemnity and the tendency to it that men try to heighten their importance by assuming severity if they have it not. For they can see that, instead of avoiding a brusque and churlish man, we estimate his integrity in proportion to his reserve, and court his confidence—till we find him out and can appraise him at his true worth. But discourtesy in the long run profits no one. The ill-tempered man has his way for a time, were it only to avoid "scenes"; but he sooner or later meets his match, and those he has bullied and frozen into compliance with his wishes will not only desert him for the new master, but will more or less recriminate on him ever after.

A mental habit, at first assumed, becomes natural in proportion as it is indulged; and the man who affects displeasure, thinking to render himself more interesting and influential thereby, will find that the less he controls his temper, the less is he able to control it. Let us clear our minds of the idea that *la brutalité*, as the French

call this national weakness, is an admirable thing.
Let us try to remember that in controversy or reproof
the rapier-thrust of the smiling, self-possessed man will
be increasingly admired as the British people leave
barbarism behind; and let us be advised that if the
retort courteous does not come readily to the tongue, it
is better to be silent and look cheerfully wise than to
deal the ungraceful knock-down blow, of which we
shall probably be afterwards ashamed, and which
rankles in the mind of the recipient out of all proportion to the injury inflicted.

In the passage given as a motto to this chapter
sagacious old John Locke shows how the powers of the
mind can be developed by practice. Is it not probable
that a *disposition* can be developed by practice as well
as a *talent* ? The Social-Democratic State will promote
cheerfulness by removing pain and privation, by breeding out disease, and by diffusing ideas ; but much also
can be done by the conscious suppression of " the old
Adam " and the cultivation of the better part of our
nature. Although cheerfulness is mainly temperamental, it must be remembered that the mind acts on
the body as well as the body on the mind. The
sprightliness of the Frenchman is partly racial, partly
a matter of cookery and digestion; but it is also
largely due to conventional usages in social intercourse.
Rousseau, Guizot, Hugo, Napoleon the Little were all
representative Frenchmen ; and they scarcely appear
to us as constitutionally cheerful men ; though I daresay in society they would have much of the unconscious
urbanity of their countrymen. The social habits of a
people become a second nature even to men of the

most widely diverse natural temperament ; and if we
would have an improvement in men's natures we must,
in addition to the material changes, seek an improvement in their manners and their social point of view.
We would do well to take a leaf out of our Gallic
brother's book, and "revise our constitution" in the
department of manners, which we have hitherto
perversely regarded as distinct from morals.

The Theosophists say there is literally a thought-
atmosphere which is affected for good or evil by even
the unexpressed thoughts of the individual, and that
the more evil thoughts he entertains, the more evil
thoughts we shall all entertain. Were this true it
would give a new and unexpected meaning to the
saying that an idea is "in the air." But without
accepting the theory that there is a physical thought-
atmosphere not cognised by the ordinary physicist, it
is safe to say that we can more or less make a thought-
atmosphere for ourselves. The mere fact that we
harbour vengeful, uncharitable, or envious thoughts
will, as a rule, show itself in our face and manner ;
and though not expressly manifested in speech, will
influence more or less the state of mind of those with
whom we come into contact. If cheerfulness and
courtesy, then, cannot be always and everywhere
evoked naturally or from altruistic motives, there still
remains the worldly-wise consideration that the more
cheerful and courteous we are ourselves, the more
likely we are to promote cheerfulness in others and to
receive courtesy at their hands. Not a very lofty
motive, to be sure ; but with human nature such as it
is (in certain parts of the world especially), who shall

say that we can afford to neglect the appeal to any legitimate form of self-interest ?

Who does not know and bless those radiant souls— men and women, young and old, the Mark Tapleys and Brothers Cherryble, the Peg Woffingtons and Walt Whitmans of every-day life — who come into our presence like sunshine in December, hypnotising and revivifying us with their contagious health and spirits ? Their advent brings hope, lifts us out of the rut of despondency, and causes us to think better of ourselves and of all mankind for the time being. While their influence remains upon us the bread tastes sweeter, the fire burns more brightly, there is more health for us in the north wind. Their path through life is one continuous illustration of the high social value of that magnetic virtue whose sober name is cheerfulness.

CHAPTER VIII.

COURAGE.

" Courage is equality to the problem—in affairs, in science, in trade, in council, or in action; [it] consists in the conviction that the agents with whom you contend are not superior in strength or resources or spirit to you."—EMERSON.

CONSIDERED as a definition, the foregoing words of Emerson fairly fill the bowl. But the brief description which we call a definition, however useful as a generalisation of facts already known, is not particularly valuable without a knowledge of the facts of which it is the categorical expression. It is of the nature of a definition to be elliptical, to omit particulars; but these are of such essential importance that the most explicit and comprehensive definition always requires illustration and explanation.

Courage is of three kinds — physical, moral and intellectual.

The physically courageous man is he who, confident in his physical powers, faces boldly dangers and difficulties that appal the person not possessed of similar confidence. The chief though not the only cause of physical cowardice is lack of experience in the use of our bodily powers, with the confidence which comes of success.

The man of moral courage is the person possessed of a strong instinct for righteousness, which may or may not be fortified by a well-grounded belief in the power of right to ultimately triumph over present difficulties. Whether moral courage is mainly intuitional, or largely rational, it arises in either case from the individual regard for morality itself. The standard of moral courage in the individual, will, therefore, depend upon the regard in which he holds the other virtues. Johnson reckoned courage " the greatest of all virtues, because unless a man has that virtue he has no security for preserving any other"; but it might with equal truth be said that the possession of the other virtues will endow us with the moral courage to defend them. What we value we shall strive to possess and shall defend when acquired. The chief cause of moral cowardice would appear to be distrust in the power of good to triumph in the long run and lack of patience to work and to wait for the moral victory. The successful prosecution of moral contention will strengthen our regard for morality : as victories are won by the way our faith in its ultimate triumph is naturally intensified.

But while patience to *wait* for the moral victory may be strengthened by practice, another species of courage is frequently required to enable us to *work* for it—namely, intellectual courage.

It is not unlikely that this last may be reckoned a philosophical alien. It is customary to speak of physical courage and of moral courage : but I am not aware that the phrase intellectual courage is ever used except in a literary way as one of the niceties of language. Intellectual "daring" is not uncommon, though it is questionable if the expression is used in a philosophical sense with the idea that it covers a

F

distinct mental attribute (which may be moral in its outcome). The tripartite division would, however, appear to be necessary. For it is clear that many persons possessed of physical and moral courage are incapable of facing up large and complex problems. In defending the right, many a man of strong moral instincts is subject to mental perturbation in which he conceives amiss, flounders in statement, or falls back upon platitudes; whereas the man of intellectual courage, confident in his power to resolve the problem into its parts, moves collectedly through the maze of considerations, excluding the extraneous, reconciling the seeming-contradictory, curtailing here, enlarging there, and effecting a demonstration by giving the factors their proper places and proportions.

The man of physical courage cannot explain, but is willing to fight. The man of merely moral courage, also unable to explain, deplores his opponents' lack of intuitive vision, and probably attributes motives, which is said to be the vice of rectitude. The man of intellectual courage neither blusters nor laments. He explains. Having safely travelled the road before, he is not afraid to set out on it again. Obviously, then, the principal cause of intellectual cowardice is lack of knowledge and reasoning power.

It may, however, be said that no courage is shown where no risk is run. But risk *is* involved in all physical, moral, and mental struggles. Only, that which makes the physically courageous man is his tendency to overrate his own strength, spirit, and resource, or to underrate the strength, spirit, and resource of his antagonist. In like manner, the man of moral courage can never be quite sure that he has not overrated the power of good to assert itself in his hands, and that disappointment, failure, and ridicule will not be his portion. Again, the man of intellectual courage may find the problem more difficult than he imagined, his logic may halt or altogether fail him, or in controversy the opposing dialectician may be more subtle or unscrupulous than he expected. But in all three cases a full knowledge of the danger and the difficulty may at most be only a mild and momentary deterrent, a reason for greater caution in the onset, or a whet to the desire for success. The physically courageous man does not require to be certain of success before essaying the feat. And this is where Emerson's definition falls short. Admiring physical bravery, he is willing to run the hazard in his desire to emulate it ; and the same holds good of the morally and intellectually courageous men with their respective ideals. The courageous act, of course, implies danger. We do not give a person credit for courage because he is equal to climbing the stairs to his bedroom. Though in a certain bodily condition the ascent may be attended with considerable *difficulty*, ordinarily there is no special *danger* attending it. But let the house take fire ; and to ascend the stairs for the purpose of rescuing a child, an invalid, or someone overpowered by the smoke fumes, will be recognised as courageous in the extreme. Even were the element of risk not present to the man of physical courage—even if he could be quite certain that he was equal to the venture—his equality would be a virtue nevertheless. Because although *he* is equal to it, other men are not. The men of merely moral and

mental courage, for instance, are not equal to it. Even
if there were no danger to him, with his eye and nerves
and muscles trained and equipped for the effort, the
fact that there is danger to others not similarly endowed
shows that he is possessed of qualities sufficiently
special to distinguish him from his fellows. The sum
of those qualities is courage.

The standards of the new ethic have nothing to do
with how a virtue is evolved. They test character
solely by results. So that even if courage come quite
natural and easy to the individual; even if by his
training and circumstances the courageous act cost
no special bodily exertion or effort of the will—his
qualities of body or mind or both constitute a virtue
all the same. For the social outcome of courage, however evolved, is in the main unquestionably valuable
and admirable, even to-day; though it is largely
displayed in the commercial game of beggar my
neighbour.

Whilst the courageous act presupposes danger, the
running of unnecessary risks is mere recklessness where
it is not bravado. It is related that at the investment
of Gradisca the French troops being allowed time to
have their dinner, refused to quit the ground, but
established their cookery under the cannons of the
place, and there ate their meal. As there was nothing
to lose by falling back, the risk of remaining within
range would only be run by men intoxicated with
success, who had forgotten prudence as a result of
long-continued familiarity with death, and the contempt
for it which would arise from an idea that we possess
an immunity from the fate we see befalling others.

Such acts show culpable recklessness rather than commendable courage. Those who gaily face danger because they do not realise it are really less courageous than those who, fully realising the danger, face it nevertheless.

Much of what was said in a previous chapter regarding the temperamental basis of cheerfulness applies equally to courage. Brave men are born rather than made; though training also can do much, as the Spartans showed. A lusty, full-blooded physique will incline a man to feats of daring and enduring; and if, as is likely, he keeps the company of those like-minded with himself, his courage will be intensified by frequent tests, and by the example and associated sentiment of his "set." Similarly, the man of moral courage will have a mind so constituted that examples of moral excellence will appeal most readily to it; whilst the man of intellectual courage will have a natural turn for logic, not necessarily of the schools, combined perhaps with intellectual curiosity, or an appetite for information.

The instinctive nature of physical courage is shown by the stand which mothers have been known to make on behalf of their children against wild animals or human assailants. The present writer has seen an under-sized Highland woman thrash a six-foot man with a rolling-pin—the man being drunk but not magnanimous—a case which finds a parallel in the defence of her chicks made by the domestic fowl against the lumbering retriever or more serious aggressor. There cannot be much thought of "equality to the problem" in such instances. The stand made is evidently a matter of automatic maternal instinct rather than reasoned confidence in her power to repel the enemy.

The instinctive quality of moral courage is attested by the refusal of the moral champion to give up his point in spite of representations, which he cannot combat, as to the folly of his position.

That intellectual courage has also an instinctive basis is shown by the tenacity of the rationalist in the face of temporarily successful opposition, and his tendency to come up with a fresh argument when the ground seems to have been taken from under his feet.

While for the sake of distinction, physically, morally, and intellectually courageous men are here dealt with as different types, in real life all the three varieties of courage are frequently found allied in the same person. John Howard, facing a whole world on the question of prison reform, going into dens of disease and turbulence, quelling the riot in Savoy Prison when the military jailers were afraid to venture near it, defending successfully against pirates the vessel in which he was a passenger, scorning kings, invading a country when denied a passport and forbidden admission by the authorities, and sitting down to convert Christendom by his writings, first, on the prisons, and, later, on the plague—here was a splendid combination of physical, moral, and intellectual courage used for the noblest and most disinterested objects. And, however high may be the place of John Howard among the galaxy of heroes, he does not by any means stand alone in the particular combination of his qualities.

Courage of all three kinds depends primarily on the state of the nervous system. The sedentary, anæmic person is always nervous; and the nervous person is usually deficient in physical and certain kinds of mental and moral courage. The typical student, spending much time indoors, in solitude, and with most of the physical faculties more or less dormant, is naturally not possessed of the physical and mental *sang froid* of the average barbarian. Just as the indoor life of the majority of women (along with certain sex factors) produces the high-strung female who "goes off" at the sight of a rat, so similar life-habits produce the man who is afraid to cross a field in which there are cattle, who flies into a hysteria of anger on slight provocation, who becomes incoherent before an audience, whose nervous flutter will not permit him to patiently combat prejudice or malignancy, who might be capable of throwing away his life in a frenzy of enthusiasm or despair, but is incapable of fencing with enemies, biding his time, and beating opposition by slow degrees, But all these social qualities of which the neurotic man is deprived are frequently met with in the man of ordinary mental gifts, provided he is possessed of enough blood and bone and muscle to command his nerves.

Though one is annoyed to see cycling and football made the serious business of so many people's lives, one ought to be still more annoyed to see men riding short distances in cabs and cars when they could walk with advantage; spending their evenings and Sundays indoors in merely recreative reading, frequently interrupted by conjugal consultations on domestic economy; to see them turning from the desk of business to the music-stand of pleasure, from the office to the theatre or public house, and never seeing a field or wood or mountain save from the windows of a railway train. We are all so dreadfully narrow and specialised to-day ! * The people who least need athletics— masons, bricklayers, bagmen, butchers, gardeners, gamekeepers—are the people who indulge most in sport and athletics ; whereas the lawyers and their clerks, compositors, journalists, shop people, and others following sedentary pursuits — who need athletics most—form the class who least readily resort to outdoor exercises, in spite of occasional pressing physical admonitions. The sporting and athletic people have no *intellectual* conscience ; the reading and musical and " domestic " men have no *physical* conscience (the last type thinking he has done his duty to his body if he takes a turn with the bassinette, poor fellow !). The lack of knowledge and mental training accounts for Quinion's preference for sports : in his leisure hours, if he is to be saved from sleep, he must see something going forward ! On the other hand, the aversion of " the pale cit " to outdoor exercise arises partly from the fact that he has received no physical training at school, and has not those bodily instincts that make the active man flee

* A hundred years ago, and less, the provincial shopkeeper kept open later at night; but it was no uncommon thing for him to shut shop in the middle of the day, leaving a notice in the window announcing that he had " Gone to the bowling-green ; will be back at five."

the precincts of the house to avoid dyspepsia, head-
ache, and ill-temper, as well as to humour the positive
craving he feels for the motion, the freer coursing of
the blood, the thrill and exuberance of all the physical
senses.

The coming social order will further physical
courage by giving the youth of both sexes physical
education. In the society of the future, gymnastics
will occupy something like the position they occupied
in ancient Greece. And the abundant leisure of after
life, with its possibility of adventure by flood and field,
will enable them to maintain the physical perfection
of which the foundations were laid in early life. There
will doubtless always be a proportion of bookworms—
of what in college slang used to be known as " saps "
and " swots " and " mugsters." But public opinion,
combined with the physical training of early life,
will act as a healthy corrective to excessive literary
indulgence.

The Social-Democratic State will further moral
courage by removing the reasons for moral subserviency. The man of to-day " lies low " where
many a time he would fain raise his voice against
cruelty and injustice—his silence arising from the
dread of economic consequences. Both physical and
moral independence will be encouraged by the feeling
that no material harm can come to others by your
making a stand and living a man's life. In one of
his tales of Indian military life, Kipling shows how
the fear of social consequences makes cowards of
men constitutionally brave. Captain Gadsby, an ideal
soldier till he marries, begins to funk at the thought

of what might befall his wife and children if his horse were to stumble on the parade ground, with the whole troop coming thundering up behind. By ensuring that widows and children will be provided for should the worst come, the male citizens of the future will find it possible to be *men* as well as husbands and fathers.

The Social-Democratic State will promote intellectual courage by affording its men and women an education at least as good as that obtained by the most favoured to-day. Instead of training men to be efficient producers only, or giving them what is known as " a good commercial education," the society of the future will recognise that man is a reasoning and an æsthetic animal, and that the culture which makes him a better man to look at and to live and work with, a more efficient citizen and a better companion to himself, is the only culture worthy of the name. With " authority " in matters of opinion largely weakened by this diffusion of culture, intellectual courage will look up generally as it has not been able to do hitherto.

In the lines in " Leaves of Grass " headed " Me Imperturbe," Walt Whitman expresses a desire to stand " at ease in nature, master of all or mistress of all, aplomb in the midst of irrational things, imbued as they, passive, receptive, silent as they ; " to be " self-balanced for contingencies, to confront night, storms, hunger, ridicule, accidents, rebuffs, as the trees and animals do." This is neither possible nor desirable. The average Englishman is sufficiently wooden already. The least intellectual human being, possessing memory, reason, and imagination as the beasts do not, would necessarily.be more subject to anticipate and fear actual danger, because he would remember past hurts and dangers, and have power to calculate threatened ones, as "the trees and animals" cannot. But a healthy absorption in widely varied pursuits, a more out-of-doors life, ideal dwellings and workplaces, care for the morrow banished, and the heartiest social fellowship in the home and outside of it, should secure the nearest *desirable* approximation to the aplomb of the wild animal.

But, it may be said, granting that nerves have been over-stimulated in the civilised man, is there not an offset of gain to the evils of this ? Are not "nerves" an important element in the composition of our great self-sacrificing social workers ? Nay, is it possible to have certain forms of genius without "nerves" ? Is not nervous exaltation necessary to the best work of the artist ? I can answer only after the manner of a lay observer. It may be necessary to the best work of some artists, as it was to the Irish patriotic editor in " Alton Locke " who could not write a leader until he had lashed himself into a passion ; but I am inclined to question whether it is necessary to the best work of the *best* artists. Here and there men of rare intellectual gifts—such as Heine and Carlyle—owe much of their power and charm to "moods" which were probably due to nerves more than to intellect pure and simple, if we may speak of such a thing. But Chaucer, Shakespeare, Goethe, Scott, and Morris could scarcely be described as chronically nervous men. A high mental tension would appear to be inseparable from certain forms of composition ; and

excitement, I should think, is indispensable to the
orator. But cannot the occasion command the mood?
or is it necessary that it should be a habitual bodily
and mental state with the orator and the poet? I
cannot give all my reasons for saying so ; but I think
not. The physically strong man, able to repress
excitement as a rule, produces greater effects by his
oratory when he *does* give the rein to his passion
than the person who is habitually a man of starts
and sighs and easily provoked outbursts of fervour.
But even if " nerves " were to the artist more than
has ever been claimed for them, that would be no
argument why neurotic tendencies should be allowed
to run riot among men and women generally. The
man of the future will not be a " logic-crushing
machine," according to the Huxleyan ideal, any more
than Huxley was himself; but neither will he weep
because he is " unable to live up to his blue china,"
nor will he bite his wife at the breakfast table because
the coffee is too strong. The world will always be
composed mainly of average people ; and although
the average will be much higher in the coming time,
it will be higher *physically* and morally as well as
mentally. That is to say, the muscle, bone, and blood
will keep the nerves in control. And of this control
courage in all its forms will be one of the fruits.

CHAPTER X.

TRUTHFULNESS.

"Our intelligence being by no other way to be convey'd to one another but by speaking, who falsifies that, betrays publick society. 'Tis the only way by which we communicate our thoughts and wills; 'tis the interpreter of the soul, and if that deceive us we no longer know, nor have no further tie upon, one another. If that deceive us, it breaks all our correspondence and dissolves all the ties of government."— MONTAIGNE.

I HAVE asked several acquaintances the question, " Why should we not tell lies ? " and although I am as fortunate in my friends—on the score of their mental calibre—as most people, I have rarely got anything like a satisfactory answer. Some replied, " Because lying is dishonourable," without saying how or why it is so ; others naïvely said, " Because it is very disgraceful when you are found out" ; while a Churchman reminded me, with an air of finality, that the bearing of false witness was forbidden by the Ninth Commandment. That thorn in the flesh to the Scottish youth of both sexes, the Shorter Catechism, usually gives " reasons "— invariably the wrong ones — for the " commands " it imposes ; but no " reasons " are given for the Ninth Commandment, not even the bribe or the threat which in these cases does duty for a reason ; and a great many worthy people appear to have taken the ethic of the dogmatic "Thou shalt not" as sufficiently self-evident to need no thought or examination for its ˎproper understanding. Whilst the instinct against falsehood happily existed before the command, and would continue to exist were the entire Decalogue to be discarded as such, it is nevertheless desirable that reasons should be forthcoming for our moral standards as for everything else of importance. Already we have writers* declaring that moral rules condemning theft, lying, unchastity, and so on, "are doctrines established by the strong for the government of the weak" (as if that were any objection to the rules); and we have had at least one protest against "the decay of lying."† It is clear that we cannot afford to dispense with any—even the scantiest—aid to morality.

Lying is anti-social on the obvious ground that a society of liars would be a society in which all social and progressive energy would be paralysed through the individual having no faith in his neighbour's word —a collapse of social confidence well illustrated by that lesson-book friend, the story of the boy who cried " wolf."

Some one has whimsically classified falsehoods into " The lie, the damned lie, and the statistical lie," the

* Among others, Mr. Van Buren Denslow, "Modern Thinkers" (with an introduction by R. G. Ingersoll).

† "The Decay of Lying: a Protest." By Oscar Wilde, *Nineteenth Century*, January, 1889. This is a sparkling and suggestive article, with much that is true in reference to art; but considered as a joke (if intended as such), a very questionable one.

three varieties being evidently graded in the order of their enormity. It would be difficult to improve on this statement in the matter of pungency; but it might, perhaps, be amended in the interests of didactic utility. I should be inclined to divide untruths into—the lie, the artistic lie, and the intellectual lie.

The case against mere direct falsehood—the lie of convenience, prudence, or fear—is plain enough, and does not require elaboration. Do not let us forget that we live "in model England," where a man's word is his bond, and where, as foreign critics, with an eye on the British book-market, say, a favourite expression of the common people is "Honour bright." After all, truthfulness and honesty are in the ordinary concerns of life oftener assumed than questioned. The bulk of the transactions of commerce take integrity (within limits) for granted. If all made-up goods had to be weighed or measured in the presence of the buyer; if all metals had to be assayed in changing hands; if we could not take the word of the vendor as to the quantity, quality, and market price of many of our purchases, life would be hopelessly intolerable. As it is, we send money thousands of miles to men we have never seen, and if it be for goods we have to get, from long experience we expect them to come to hand; or if the money be sent for value we have received, we look for the postman to bring the receipted bill in due course, and would be surprised if it were withheld and the claim presented a second time. Scarcely anywhere except in novels does the merchant ring every coin on the counter or weigh it in finely-adjusted scales. We do not check every item

of every bill sent us ; neither—although scamping has
been heard of in the nineteenth century—do we look
narrowly into the innermost and hidden parts of every
piece of work done for us. In spite of our army of
inspectors, policemen, and analysts, it may even to-
day be fairly said that the greatest rogues are not
always as mendacious and knavish as they might be.
Human nature, for all the cynics and humourists say
about it, shows a wonderful power of bearing up and
holding out against adverse circumstances.

By the artistic lie is meant the comparatively
innocent and frequently entertaining falsehood vended
for the purpose of improving a story in the telling or
heightening the importance of the teller. Of this class
a well known example is Falstaff's " men in buckram "
—a species of falsehood the more harmless because so
few would be taken in by it. Then there is the flighty
public man who keeps close at hand some abstruse
and awe-inspiring book, which, when visitors call, he
has "just been reading." Again, there is the person
who invites you to dinner, assuring you that you must
" take pot luck " ; and when the event comes off you
find that pot luck means ten courses (exclusive of the
coffee and cigars), and two hours spent at table—a
display for which the poor soul has been preparing for
a fortnight, and thinks to pass off as his normal style
of living. William Pitt, with his swathes of flannel
and his crutches dramatically disposed ; Emerson,
with his notes hidden among the flowers on the
dinner-table, while he palms off the carefully conned
and premeditated periods as extempore oratory ; or,
to class common artists with the great ones, the

sportsman who comes home with boasts of his prowess
and a brace of fine trout "caught" at the fishmonger's
" for a consideration "—all these afford specimens of
the artistic and not always conscious falsehood. Not
an unpleasant form of untruthfulness perhaps, nor
strikingly anti-social in its consequences, but carrying
its absurd penalties all the same.

But the spirit of truth surely requires us, not only
to avoid deliberate falsehood, plain or artistic, but
also to guard against the mental looseness which
permits us to propagate errors of which we are partly
conscious. In making up our minds and adopting a
certain position, the most deliberate of us are shame-
fully off-hand and sophistical in one respect or another.
One can quite understand that a certain sub-logical
process may go on in the mind very rapidly, and
that upon many matters a fairly sound opinion may
be formed without going through a full and formal
process of reasoning. But an element of danger
always attends the settlement of questions by this
sub-logical process. In fact, in the minds of many
persons it might be said that decisions are arrived at
by a process which is all "sub" and no logic. The
average man, and still more the average woman, will
frequently adopt opinions—especially in connection
with important matters—upon grounds which are an
outrage on the ethics of belief. The unreasoning
opposition offered to new ideas, subsequently adopted
with acclamation, is sufficient to show that at all
times there exists a majority holding opinions which
it has no *intellectual* right to hold; that many who
would scorn to tell a downright lie are guilty of the

falsehood of pursuading themselves that a proposal which they have never properly examined is dangerous or unsound, or, on the other hand, safe and sound; for society *accepts* ideas on the wrong grounds as well as rejects them. How seldom things come about *as* they ought, *when* they ought, and for the right reasons! But with intellectual dishonesty so universally common, is it any wonder that life should be such a purgatory to the wise?

It is impossible to say with truth that this mendacity of the intellect is confined to the illiterate. The most erudite are unlearned as regards something or another; though that does not prevent them from forming erroneous opinions, dogmatically held, about matters of which they have no adequate knowledge. Readers of Boswell will remember those conversations between Johnson and his friends in which the great Samuel bullies his hearers into acquiescence with arguments through which a very average man could to-day drive the proverbial coach and six. It was remarked by one of the circle that if the doctor's pistol flashed in the pan he could always knock down an opponent with the butt end of it. What is this but an admission that the Great Cham of literature persisted in holding opinions which he could not fairly defend, and that when cornered he would browbeat an adversary rather than own his error and abandon it? No other explanation is possible. For one cannot imagine a dialectician like Johnson being at a loss for argument to defend a position legitimately held. If Johnson could be largely guilty of this sort of evasion of the truth, how much more guilty must less intellectual people be! The prevalence of this disloyalty to truth is reflected in the statement by a modern critic that "It is so easy to convert others: so difficult to convert one's self." This simply means that we do not scruple to persuade other people by arguments whose soundness and validity we have not yet settled in our own minds.

From intellectual tergiversation we suffer more and have more to fear than from the mendacities of the conscious liar, whose operations are largely rendered innocuous by his being frequently found out, and his statements liberally discounted ever afterwards. And so far as I have noticed, it is precisely the plain, honest people, least likely to indulge in deliberate falsehood, who are most given to intellectual dishonesty. For plain people have a strong tendency to intellectual laziness, and as opinions, right or wrong, *have* to be formed on large and complex questions, these mental sluggards are as often in the wrong as not. The regular hatchet-thrower is, on the contrary, usually rather a sprightly and ingenious person, and on large questions may well be right oftener than wrong.

Now, as before indicated, I attach more importance to truthfulness in great than in small matters. If the man who has a regard for great general truths is sometimes less precise in ordinary converse, his inaccuracy proceeds, not so much from a desire to falsify as from mere inattention to, or impatience of, details. We are required to tell the truth, but it is only upon oath that we are required to tell the *whole* truth. The person who can balance accounts to a farthing is a very admirable citizen in his way, and the verbosely accurate legal document is not without its advantages; but pedantic accuracy is not the thing most needed in civilised communities to-day.

The cumulative character of the virtues appears very strikingly in connection with truthfulness. The higher the degree in which we possess the other virtues the higher will be the degree in which we shall possess the virtue of truthfulness. For a drunkard, a sluggard, a sloven, or a coward to be truthful is difficult in the extreme; for not only are there past lapses to cover up by falsehood, but to the coward at least there is a constant temptation to escape positions in which courage will be required. But to the person who is brave, chaste, temperate, diligent, and careful, truthfulness comes easy, inasmuch as there are few past sins of omission or commission to conceal and few evil consequences to fear in the future.

If the artistic liar is not to be deterred by the consideration that he takes no one in, let him go on, and bless him. All that we can add is that the person addicted to extravaganza makes his legitimate talents very cheap by his exercises in this line. We all know men of genuine parts whose serious speech and action are enormously discounted on this very ground. The wag, the caricaturist, the *poseur* is aways underrated by his fellows—even when his counsel is wiser than that of the solemn and stolid person. And after all, there is some warrant for this discounting of the persistent hyperbolist. One gets impatient with the jackanapes who is eternally casting about for a joke at whatever sacrifice of taste or truth. Life is not a jest any more than it is a tragedy ; and we feel that there is something slack and shallow about a person who is everlastingly on the grin. It is possible to reap much fine and quiet enjoyment from men and things, without continually calling upon our friends to join us in extravagant hilarity at the latest "good thing," perhaps of our own invention.

The penalty which the artistic liar has to pay is that no one will take him seriously even when he wishes it. I know a big, fat Irishman, the very essence of fun and good nature, who, although suffering much sickness and pain, has won for himself such a reputation among his friends as a humourist and a man of inspired mendacity, that when he really needs their sympathy they can only laugh in his face even as he recounts his woes. The character we frequently assume has a tendency to become our real character ; and even if it does not become so in reality it may be a grave matter that it should do so in appearance. The falling back upon canards and fables to render oneself interesting or amusing indicates either poverty of experience, reading, and observation, or else incapacity to make the truth entertaining. Cultivate the power to describe what you have verily seen and heard in a fairly eventful and observant career, and you need not envy the gifted Munchausen.

Socialism will further the virtue of plain truthfulness by abolishing shop, office, and counting-house lies, and the lies of hypocrisy and sycophancy, and, by breeding better animals—men of a prouder spirit—it will breed men with more of the instinct of honour that forbids falsehood. Lying is anti-social because of its effects on our neighbours, but it is also anti-social by reason of its effects on the individual himself. The person who takes refuge in falsehoods develops an invertebrate habit of escaping consequences instead of facing them up. Evading difficulties instead of sur- mounting them, he (or she) loses the wholesome discipline and development which trial and effort afford. The man who dodges his responsibilities by resorting to a lie, not only hurts his fellows by the consequences of his act, but the immediate act hurts himself: he stands lower in his own estimation; his self-reliance and usefulness are impaired; and, properly considered, the less use a man is to himself, the less use is he to society. The quality of courage is enormously helped by truthfulness. Those who tell the truth and accept the consequences will be the better for their bravery, and will find it easier to dare the second time than it was the first. In the words of Emerson : " The permanent interest of every man is never to be in a false position, but to have the weight of nature to back him in all he does." Or, as was said by Jamie Fleeman, the Laird of Udny's fool, after he had tried the other thing, " The truth aye tells best."

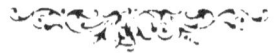

CHAPTER XI.

HONESTY.

"If I steal money from any person, there may be no harm done by the mere transfer of possession; he may not feel the loss, or it may prevent him from using the money badly. But I cannot help doing this great wrong towards man, that I make myself dishonest. What hurts society is not that it should lose its property, but that it should become a den of thieves; for then it must cease to be society. This is why we ought not to do evil that good may come; for at any rate this great evil has come that we have done evil and are made wicked thereby."— W. K. CLIFFORD.

THE virtue of honesty is in its larger accceptation bound up with so many other virtues that to dissect it by itself requires some preliminary clearing away of extraneous matter, and a definite understanding as to terms. The word honesty is used as a sort of verbal half-tone to connote a number of virtues besides that of respect for property rights. We describe one who is remarkable for truthfulness and candour as an honest man. When Mr. John Burns and Mr. John Morley were each in turn called " honest John," regard was had, not so much to their respect for other people's property as to their courageous and out-spoken hostility to institutions and ideas of which they disapproved. In like manner, we speak of a chaste

woman as an "honest" woman.* And, again, of a
piece of work which is what it professes to be we say
that it is an "honest job:" thus Carlyle speaks of the
making of "honest boots." To the extent that honesty
is bound up, in ordinary speech, with courage and
truthfulness, charity and chastity, I have already discussed it in discussing these, whilst in a subsequent
chapter I shall deal with it in relation to "Diligence."
In the present chapter I shall treat of honesty in its
limited and original sense as meaning simply respect
for the rights of property.

A discussion, from the Socialist point of view, of
honesty so specified may at first thought be equally
surprising to friends and foes. Many of the opponents
of Socialism pretend to believe—and others of them I
daresay honestly believe—that Socialists, if they do
not propose to overturn the entire Decalogue, are at
any rate quite bent on abolishing the Eighth Commandment. On the other hand, many Socialists who
have not considered what the economic life of the
future will be like, may be of opinion that respect for
property cannot be a virtue in the Social-Democratic
State, inasmuch as "property" will then be non-

---

* "*Honest* has in Scotch a peculiar application, irrespective of
any integrity of moral character. It is a kindly mode of referring
to an individual, as we would say to a stranger, 'Honest man,
would you tell me the way to——?' or as Lord Hermand [one
of the old Scottish judges of the Monboddo and Braxfield school],
when about to sentence a woman for stealing, began, remonstra-
tively: 'Honest woman, what garr'd [made] ye steal your
neighbour's tub?'" (Dean Ramsay's "Reminiscences.") Surely
there never was a more violent wresting of the word "honest"
from its primary meaning.

existent. The dictum of the Anarchist Proudhon—
" La propriété c'est le vol " (as near as can be translated, " Property is theft ")—is regarded in many
quarters as a Socialist sentiment ; and the actual social
arrangements of the future society have• been so
slightly and so seldom treated, in popular propaganda
at least, that a large number of our friends do not
know, for instance, that there is a difference between
Socialism and Communism ; that Socialism does not
imply a common store from which all can supply their
wants without hindrance, without check or waste or
abnormal acquisitiveness, and without guarantee that
the person using the store has rendered service en-
titling him to take of the goods produced by others.
Laurence Gronlund, whose " Co-operative Commonwealth " has been styled the New Testament of
Socialism (as the " Capital " is its Old Testament),
has tried to distinguish between Socialism and
Communism by describing Communism as meaning
" each according to his needs," and Socialism " each
according to his deeds." This is excellent as a
definitive distinction, especially when taken along
with Gronlund's explanation of what it means. The
trouble in connection with most definitions, as I have
previously complained, is that they are *only* definitions, and not descriptions ; that they are an attempt
to sum up in one short sentence what cannot be thus
briefly expressed. This definitive distinction of
Gronlund's is no exception to the general run of such
statements. It is possible to misunderstand it, and it
is possible not to understand it at all. The economic
institutions of the Social-Democratic State will have

so much to do with honesty that they must of necessity receive some little consideration here.

In that delightful book " News from Nowhere," Morris describes how in the society of the future two of his personages visit a communal store, and selecting a fine tobacco pouch (if my memory serves), walk off without leaving any other equivalent for it than fair words to the girl in attendance. This is Communism presented in a very simple and artistic way; but one need not be of a hopelessly commercial turn of mind to see that it would scarcely do. Doubtless there will come a time when many things will be " without money and without price," as the highways, public libraries, and water for domestic purposes are without price in the ordinary sense already, and as bread would be in Paris if the Free Bread Bill of Clovis Hugues became law. But even under the best social arrange-ments one cannot conceive of the amount of wealth being so unlimited that every citizen can be permitted to have all he can possibly want. Neither can he be left to be the sole judge of what he *needs*. If a millionaire can get into difficulties to-day by consuming or wasting more than he can pay for, surely it would be possible for the citizen of the future state to take, if allowed to do so, more than his fair share of the total wealth produced. But it is no part of the plan of Socialism to allow him to do so. In the Social-Democratic State, while generous provision will be made for the sick and helpless, the citizen will be granted an income, which will be indicated by labour checks or credit cards, as advocated by Gron-lund, Bellamy, and John Carruthers, the sagacious

economist of the future society, whose "Communal
and Commercial Economy " and " Political Economy
of Socialism " are not, I think, as well known as they
ought to be. The credits granted to the citizens will
be equal in all cases, without reference to skill, intelligence, or the nature of the service performed ; but no
credits will be given to able-bodied shirkers, who will
thus be starved into doing their share of the world's
work without other compulsion. The direction of
waste labour-force into useful channels, the compulsion on all capable persons to work, and the vastly
improved methods of production, will greatly increase
the aggregate wealth. But while the share of each
member of the community will thus be generous as
compared with the average income to-day, it will still,
of course, be limited ; and if comfort, luxury, and
pleasure be taken out by the citizen in certain
directions he must be content to forego them in
others ; though it goes without saying that many
pleasures which now cost money will then be free.

If my friend Cunninghame Graham were dissatis-
fied with the horses kept for hire at the communal
stables, and insisted on having a mustang of his very
own, of course he could have it ; but he could not
expect to have, in addition, a yacht waiting his
pleasure in the river at the bottom of the garden, or
a library of *editions de luxe* under his own roof. If
William Morris succumbed to the temptation of
Elzevirs and Baskervilles, Shakespearean quartos,
rare prints, and fine carpets, he also would have to
do without the yacht, and conduct his itinerary of
the Thames in a quite ordinary boat. If Shaw and

Walker wished to visit Venice and "do" the
Mediterranean in a craft of their own—the public
electric ships not suiting their purpose—Shaw could
not expect to also keep a carriage and a coachman
to take him round the theatres and concert rooms.
But there would, of course, be no reason why Morris
should not sail in Walker's yacht, or Shaw ride in
Mrs. Sparling's carriage, or Graham read Morris's
books. The pleasures and graces of hospitality,
treating, and the giving of gifts will not be lost to the
men and women of coming years ; and "plain living
and high thinking" will still have their warrant in the
nature of things. The dashing blades of the Social-
Democratic State will know by their punched credit
cards, or their lack of labour checks, when they are
living beyond their income, while the folk "of frugal
mind" will discover "by the same token" (as it were)
when they are failing to enjoy all that they are entitled
to, and will thus be tempted to "launch out," since
saving will be without motive.

And now what connection has all this with honesty ?
Well, it is designed to show two things mainly. First,
that outside of the socially-owned means of production
there will be abundance of private property in the
Social-Democratic State, and that even under the
equalitarian economic arrangements then existing,
there will still be room for prudence in using and
spending the wealth controlled by the individual, and
that as long as he experiences any difficulty in
gratifying his desires there will always be some slight
motive—ever so slight—for dishonesty. The other
point I wished to make clear was that the ample

remuneration of the Social-Democratic citizen, the knowledge that the resources of all are equal, and that if a fine display is made in one direction there must be retrenchment in another, will minimise the tendency to "keep up appearances" beyond our means —that prime cause of dishonesty; and that while cupidity, covetousness, and dishonesty may perhaps never be wholly eradicated, they will be weakened to practical extinction. The Arabian proverb has it that " The dust alone can fill the eye of man "; but that was not spoken of man in a Socialist community. The " kleptomaniac " habits of society dames, removed by generations of affluent ancestors from actual poverty, proves the persistence of a magpie acquisitiveness despicable enough, but not implying a very great depth of turpitude. Considering that the average woman of the well-to-do classes gets her supplies of money grudgingly; that she knows her husband, father, or brother makes his money by methods not always immaculately honest ; and that in the end the shopkeeper will come out best from their dealings, there is no need to think hard things of human nature because of these occasional petty peculations. Neither does the widespread lack of conscience in borrowers of books and umbrellas, and defrauders of the railway companies and customs and income-tax officials strike one as implying very grave moral defects ; though it *is* a matter for serious regret that people should be content to dodge the effects of a bad system rather than try to make an end of the system itself.

The first and most obvious argument against dishonesty is the chagrin inflicted on the dispossessed one by the knowledge of his loss. I daresay there are not a few persons who will hold their heads as high with another man's hat upon it as though the headgear were the result of their own honest work; but such effrontery can only proceed from a shallow cynicism which I should think is the saddest mental property a man can possess. What sort of conception can such persons have of their fellow-creatures? What amount of faith in their friends? What agonies of discomfort must they not feel when obliged to leave their property at the mercy of people whose honesty they must measure more or less by their own?

I think it will be found on mature consideration that the really great men, famous and obscure, have been signalised by, above everything else, a cheery and simple-minded social faith, which prompted them to believe that the righteousness of the thing in which they were interested would sooner or later appeal to their fellows, and come uppermost just *because* it was right. Who does not know of men, in high life and in humble, who, out of the singleness of their minds and the fulness of their social faith, have emerged victorious from frequent defeat and long misunderstanding, while Craft and Obliquity stood by amazed to find that honesty was the best policy after all. Show us a man who thinks well of his neighbours, and he will be a man who is full of the possibilities of social service.

But a man cannot think well of his neighbours if he knows they have pilfered his books, enticed his fowls to their hencote, " conveyed " the rake which he left outside the backyard gate when last he cleared out weeds from the garden. And the less a man thinks of, and believes in, his fellows, the less he will risk, and do, and suffer for them. This drying-up of the springs of altruistic feeling is the worst feature of dishonesty. To the extent that society approximates to a den of thieves, to the extent that social meanness obtains in it, it will be a society of smooth-faced cynics, thinking worse of one another than the actual circumstances justify, and altruistic effort will be correspondingly begrudged and withheld. Honour may exist among out-and-out professional thieves; Charley Bates may sincerely admire the Artful Dodger; but what fellow-feeling can there be between the seemingly respectable Jones and the seemingly respectable Brown if Brown feels that he wants to count his spoons, so to say, after Jones has gone, or if Jones believes that, had he not reminded Brown of that copy of " Daniel Deronda " he borrowed, it would never have been returned ? The sum of the petty defects and vices we dectect in one another is at the bottom of much of the easy contempt which commonplace persons reciprocally feel.

But the law of Meum and Tuum will not hold a very exalted place in the ethical code of the future. In the clamour of grown men over "my money," " my land," " my copyright," there is something reminding one of the bickerings of children over " my place in the sun " and " my seat by the fire." And yet, if the too eager assertion of rights by the owner is puerile, the hankering of the covetous one after another's property is more petty still. The argument against a too great concern about property-rights cuts both ways, applying to the determined aggressor as well as to the frenzied defender. An Individualist scoffer once borrowed my pocket-knife to sharpen a pencil. As he shut it up to return it, he pretended to think better of it, and jocularly said, "Oh, I shall keep it. It's as much mine as yours in the abstract." "But," I objected, "in the abstract it's as much mine as yours, and in the concrete it cost me a shilling."

After all, is not honesty—the sense of right of possession in the fruits of our labour—the very basis of Socialism? Is it not our primary objection to Individualism that it is a dishonest system? At bottom our movement is a recognition of the soundness of Carlyle's addition to the Eighth Commandment: "Thou shalt not be stolen from." The Socialist declares that if he had his full wages—that natural recompense of labour which Adam Smith defined as the full value of the product—there would be no interest, rent, or profit for the blackmailing monopolists; that rent, profit, interest are so many synonyms for robbery, fraud, and extortion. The boot is on the other leg, O friend the enemy! It is not we who seek to abolish the virtue of honesty, but rather, by robbing dishonesty of its motive, to give honesty, on the great scale as in the petty dealings of life, such a chance as it never has had before.

CHAPTER XII.

DILIGENCE.

"Mankind was immersed, so to say, in an atmosphere—
Nature—which, by contact, continually irritated the sensitive
extremities of the nerves. Not merely the senses, but the entire
surface of the body, both external and internal, was set at work.
The sensations imparted to it, by reverberating in the brain,
the marrow, and the nervous centres, there became transformed
into tonicity, motion, and ideas; and he [Dr. Pascal] felt
convinced that good health lay in the normal fulfilment of this
work: the reception of sensations and their ejection in the form
of motion and ideas—the nourishment, in fact, of the human
machine by the regular play of its organs. Work thus became
the great law, the regulator of the living universe."—ZOLA.

THE following passage from the opening chapter of
" Adam Bede " describes what we have all seen at
one time or another :—

All hands worked on in silence for some minutes until the
church clock began to strike six. Before the first stroke had
died away, Sandy Jim had loosed his plane and was reaching
his jacket ; Wiry Ben had left a screw half driven in, and
thrown his screwdriver into the tool-basket; Mum Taft, who,
true to his name, had kept silence throughout the previous
conversation, had flung down his hammer as he was in the act
of lifting it ; and Seth, too, had straightened his back, and
was putting out his hand towards his paper cap. Adam alone
had gone on with his work as if nothing had happened. But,
observing the cessation of tools, he looked up and said in a
tone of indignation—

H

" Look there, now ! I can't abide to see men throw away their tools i' that way the minute the clock begins to strike, as if they took no pleasure in their work, and was afraid o' doing a stroke too much."

Seth looked a little conscious, and began to be slower in his preparations for going, but Mum Taft broke silence and said—

" Ay, ay, Adam lad, ye talk like a young 'un. When ye are six-an'-forty like me, istid o' six-an'-twenty, ye wonna be so flush o' workin' for nought."

" Nonsense," said Adam, still wrathful ; " what's age got to do with it, I wonder ? Ye arena getting stiff yet, I reckon. I hate to see a man's arms drop down as if he was shot, before the clock's fairly struck, just as if he'd never a bit o' pride and delight in's work. The very grindstone 'ull go on turning a bit after you loose it."

In his desire to see men interested in, and pleased with, their work, one feels that Adam is right. We may detest Capitalism, believe in Trade Unionism and Socialism, aud still approve of hearty and intelligent work in a short working day. To be opposed to Capitalism does not mean that we should be mere "eye servants," energetic only when an overseer is looking on. If Capitalism is unjust to us, that is no reason why we should be unjust to ourselves. Even if the fruits of our energy and interest in our work do benefit chiefly the capitalist, our feeling of integrity to our own powers makes one rebel against allowing oneself to become a recreant and a skulker. And yet there is much to be said for the qualified industrial ardour of Mum Taft and the others.

One of the many grudges that the worker has against Commercialism is that it has done so much to make industry hateful. By excessive hours of labour, the frequent ugliness, monotony, and unworthiness of the work itself, and the feeling on the part of the artisan that he is shabbily paid, an instinct against work is developed. Indeed, the aversion to work hard, to do more than one is paid for, is something more than an instinct. It is, to a certain extent, grounded in reason. The casual worker, taken on for the job, and paid by time, knows that the harder he works the sooner the job will be finished. The regular " hand " dreads to do more than is necessary (he says) lest the staff should be reduced and he be one of those selected to go. Neither the one nor the other takes readily to the idea of providing work for all by a steady, progressive shortening of the hours. Hence the " rusher " in a workshop is viewed with contempt and dislike. Where the work is done by time, the introduction of a man who is believed to be a " pacemaker " will sometimes provoke a strike. The marking of a " 'stab " compositor's copy, so that the amount of his work can be accurately measured, is forbidden by the rules of the Typographical Association, as are also task work and " timing." It is stated that some unions specifically limit the output per man ; but I know of no instances of this. While, however, the specific limitation of each man's pro-duction may be questioned, there can be no doubt at all about the general tendency to discourage "rushing" on time work. The deterrents employed to this end are defended by the trade unionist on the ground that work is thus provided for a greater number of men ; but it is difficult to believe that he is mainly actuated by consideration for others. The worker in constant

employment has, as a rule, small concern for the
unemployed, and is ready enough to repeat the often
gratuitous sneer about "men who don't want work."
He will not risk much to secure reduction of the
hours of labour; and, while he condemns piecework
and overtime, he is prompt enough to accept both if
the terms are favourable.

The fact is, the average man has no great fondness
for application, either close or intense. I have seen
workmen put themselves to more trouble to evade
an overseer's eye when shirking than it would have
cost them to remain at work ; though, to be sure,
the effort would afford a change, would, as is said,
" break the monotony." The outdoor worker likes
an occasional smoke and a chat in the course of the
day, and, when opportunity offers, is not averse to an
adjournment to the nearest public house. Painters
and plumbers flirt with the servant girls, and
succumb to the temptation of a cold collation below
stairs when "the coast is clear." Compositors take
snuff with one another ; and tea, both before and after
noon, is not unknown in the printing office. This
blending of work and play is not by any means
confined to those whose hours are long and whose
labour is tedious. The bank teller, whose hours are
short, and whose labour is not exactly mechanical,
chats over the broad counter with depositors;
merchants have their "snacks" and "nips" at
frequent intervals during business hours ; and they,
as well as the lawyers (whose hours are usually from
about ten to four), have many a gossip with callers
on matters far removed from either commerce or the

law. This is, of course, as it should be; and he would be a hard man who would seriously object. But let it be borne in mind that all these are actuated by hopes and fears, by necessities and ambitions, such as in their *nature* at least will not operate with the man of the future ; and if they can thus relax the sinews and unbend the brows, with so much, both without and within, to urge them on with unflagging zeal and intensest concentration, what will they do when the more obvious reasons for zeal and concentration are withdrawn ?

There are many who fear, not wholly without cause if one were to judge by what may be seen in a day's walk, that the freedom from fear of want and the lack of ambition to dazzle by wealth would, in the Social-Democratic State, encourage an amount of indolence and inattention which would go far to cancel the otherwise good effects of our having got rid of landlordism, capitalism, and wasteful competition. In every great city to-day there are thousands of men, neither men of means nor yet in hopeless poverty, who are simply incapable of following, not merely any vocation of a humdrum, routine character, but incapable of regularly following any vocation whatever. Has ever anyone asked, and with any approach to completeness answered, where all the people come from who fill the law courts, who sit out the day meetings of municipal councils, who swarm in the public reading-rooms, and who attend the debates in ordinaries of the Cogers Hall type ? They are not so much business men who have "looked in for half-an-hour," nor workmen temporarily out of a job.

They are neither invalids nor elderly men living on
annuities or their savings. They are, in the main,
simply incorrigible idlers. Their wives or widowed
mothers keep shops, laundries, lodging-houses, or
brothels ; or they live on their grown-up sons and
daughters ; or they are petty speculators, petty commission agents, artistic begging-letter writers, or
common sponges. These men despise the ordinary
workman, nor do they exactly envy the busy professional man or trader. The well-to-do man with a
hobby which costs him money and trouble they
regard with mild wonder and amused contempt. I
have more than once heard representatives of this
order say that no man possessed of *nous* need go into
a workshop or work hard anywhere to earn a living.

Of course, these nondescripts would find it impossible to live in such absolute idleness in the
Social-Democratic State (though there would still be
relations to prey upon), even supposing—what is
unlikely—that any of the generations of them lived
to see the fully-developed Social-Democratic State.
And as the hours of labour will be much shorter then
than now, in *that* respect labour will be less irksome.
But the existence of such a numerous class of inveterate
shirkers is enough to prove that in the average man
there is a strong tendency to mere idleness and aim-
lessness, which, but for the compulsions and tempta-
tions of existing circumstances, might run to great
lengths. I readily grant—and indeed urge—that the
need to busy oneself in some direction or another is
ineradicable ; that even the street-corner loafer will
lend a hand at a fire or will bustle about to help the

driver of a vehicle whose horse has come down on the paving stones. But the trouble is that, while the average man is willing to work occasionally where his choice is free, he considers his lot a hard one if necessity compels him to continue regularly at a given task. He is willing to work at almost anything save that at which he is asked to work. It is a common thing to hear even good workmen profess a dislike to their trade.

Now, as under Socialism no man can be outlawed or driven forth from a community because of negligence or incapacity or slothfulness, since it would be manifestly unfair for a community to pass on its moral rubbish to its neighbours, as is often done to-day, so diligence will require to be more spontaneous than it is now. It may be freely admitted that in the Social-Democratic State the standard of public spirit will be much higher than at present ; but we find that even in the work of parties and institutions where the labour is voluntary, where each man is on an equality with his fellows, and where something like *esprit de corps* might be expected to animate every member of the party, there are always persons who take things easy, and leave their share of the work to be done by others or not done at all, even where it is admittedly necessary. In the Social-Democratic State, where there will be no competition (in the ordinary sense) to obtain employment and no competition to keep it when obtained, by proving oneself a better man than one's neighbour, the virtue of diligence, the pride in one's powers as artificer or artist, the feeling of integrity to ourselves and loyalty to the State—that

is, our neighbours and friends—these allied qualities
will be of the highest importance, of infinitely more
importance than they are meanwhile, when a man's
slothfulness or carelessness merely injure his chance of
retaining his employment or keep down his employer's
bank account.

In old-established, easy-going businesses it is quite
marvellous how leisurely will be the movements of a
man who has been long in the service, or how con-
servative in his methods of working he will become.
Where the tenure of office is secure, and there is no
great call upon the worker for the display of activity
or originality in his work, matters show a tendency to
drop into a jog-trot style of working which strikes a
new-comer with amazement. Every man looks upon
himself as an exception. He thinks if there are any
favours agoing, if anybody is to be allowed to take it
easy, he is the man. So-and-So and Such-and-Such,
he can see, are at their posts there all right, and it is
what ought to be, of course ; but he is not in the
mood to-day, or his past services entitle him to a rest ;
and, after all, it " comes off a broad board," " a good
firm." And as most of them are reasoning from the
same premises, there is a slowing-down all round
which not only affects the quantity of work done, but
the quality also. For I have long been satisfied that
the best work, *as well* as the most of it, is done more
or less under the spur of haste.

The ideal of diligence must, therefore, be highly
pitched under Socialism, not merely because slothfulness would seriously detract from the common fund
of wealth to be shared, but because indifferentism in

service, radiating from man to man and from one branch of service to another, would so accumulate in all departments of social activity as to paralyse progress and reduce society to the condition of an elderly person who, having done good work in his time, now lives a fat and easy life on the strength of past achievements, hoping all things and believing all things except that greater efforts can be required from himself.

The lack of personal diligence will be regarded as anti-social because it incapacitates the sluggard from doing good work even when he has a mind to, whilst it puts him in arrears and indebtedness to his fellows. The skulker is necessarily driven into concealment, hypocrisy, and makeshift—for the vices are cumulative in character as well as the virtues—and he thus not only robs his neighbours by his spiritless movements, but becomes an exemplar of evil to all around him.

How, then, it may be asked, is diligence to be kept alive in the Social-Democratic State ? You hint that the shortening of the hours of labour will not be enough ; will it not, then, be enough that the citizen will feel he is working for himself as a member of the body social, and that the more he produces the more he as a member of the body social will enjoy ?

That certainly ought to be an incentive to diligence ; but I am of opinion that something further will be required and will grow up naturally. What this additional incentive is and how it will arise I shall presently try to show.

Bellamy gets over the difficulty of occasional

inherent laziness by the dogmatic assumption that " service is rather a matter of course than of compulsion. . . . It is regarded as so absolutely natural and reasonable that the idea of its being compulsory has ceased to be thought of. He would be thought to be an incredibly contemptible person who should need compulsion in such a case. Nevertheless, to speak of service being compulsory would be a weak way to express its absolute inevitableness. Our entire social order is so wholly based upon and deduced from it that if it were conceivable that a man could escape it he would be left with no possible way to provide for his existence. He would have excluded himself from the world, cut himself off from his kind, in a word, committed suicide." In another part of his excellent and usually persuasive book, Bellamy shows how, by the grading of the industrial army and the pressure of public opinion, the pace is made, if anything, too hot for the young men of the twenty-first century.

He makes out a very fair case ; but somehow or other it does not seem to carry complete conviction. I may be unduly " reading the conditions of the present into the future ; " but at least I know working men better than our good friend Bellamy does, which is perhaps my misfortune, but certainly not his fault. In any case, my belief is that the hope of promotion will not be found so strong an inducement to diligence as the author of " Looking Backward " appears to believe. An industrial army cannot consist of officers; it must in the main be made up of privates ; and the great bulk of the population will be quite content to remain privates, and their share of public opinion will not be calculated to goad on the recruit to rise to a higher grade, but rather to induce him to rest content with being what they themselves are. Public opinion is, as a rule, simply the opinion of our own particular set ; and if we are inclined to take it easy and let others do the "rushing" we shall always find plenty of people of a similar mind to encourage and confirm us in our bent.

One idea does not seem to have occurred to Bellamy ; and it is of such importance in this connection that his omission of it can surely proceed only from the fact that he is not a craftsman ; that, dealing with *ideas* and *words* as distinguished from *things*, he has no notion of the need of art in labour if it is to be pleasant. For myself, I am satisfied that unless the men of the future are able to enjoy the pleasures of creative effort, unless they are able to express something of their own taste, their individuality, in their work, they may well be less diligent than even the fear-driven drudge of to-day. Adam Bede might well vie with Mum Taft in his aversion to labour if he had to feed a machine in some vast joinery works where *tools* have lost their use (save to the engineer), and where hand and eye are no longer required to plan and cut and carve and fit, but only to tend *machines*, which, instead of aiding the hand, supersede it. We send lads to school to get a smattering of some six or eight subjects ; and on going to "work" they find they have studied literature and science in order to qualify them to look after nuts and screws and cylinders.

It is no wonder if it be reckoned a waste of time for a

young man of parts to remain at the carpenter's bench
or the compositor's frame. The great mania possessing
young and old alike to-day is to make all clever workmen into clerks, salesmen, overseers, or bagmen. Let
a compositor, say, be quick and accurate at his work,
and show some general intelligence, with, it may be, a
certain literary faculty, and his friends will tell him
he is a fool to waste his time at a case of types. And
what they say he has long before begun to think.
Moved by no ambition to make his trade worthy of
such men as he conceives himself to be in respect of
hours, wages, the character of the work itself, and
the places in which he and others have to do it, he
begins to look around for an opening as a reporter, a
press corrector, or at the very least a lino. operator.
That is to say, he is anxious to throw up the useful
work he can really do for some work for which he is
in all probability less fitted, and which in any case
is not worthier work than that which he is doing. As
if any man could be too clever or know too much to
be a printer! It is a poor craft indeed that is not
worthy of the best man who ever tried to master it.
Commend me to the spirit of the shoemaker of whom
an American preacher speaks:

> I asked a cobbler once how long it took to become a good
> shoemaker. He answered promptly, "Six years, and then you
> must travel." That cobbler had the artist-soul. I told a friend
> the story, and he asked his cobbler the same question. "How
> long does it take to become a good shoemaker?" "All your life,
> sir." That was better—a Michael Angelo of shoes!

The making of *things* is despised to-day. There
never was a time—no, absolutely never—when men

cared less for the common processes of industry. Men
want to exploit labour; they want to sell goods; they
want to make money and live easily. But so long as
they can make money they do not seem to care what
they *do*, what they work at; nor do they even care so
much what they *have* for their money so long as they
have plenty of it. Men of means live in jerry houses;
they wear shoddy clothes; their boots and furniture
are machine made; their newspapers are vilely printed
on trashy foreign paper; their books—if they bother to
keep a library—are rarely bound, but come to them
and stay with them in the publisher's temporary
machine-made cases, they knowing not that anything
better is needed or can be had. They actually do not
know how to spend their money—have no idea of the
good things that are to be had for it. Those are
the things they will *have* and *use;* but what of the
things they will *do ?* Well, imagine a man wishing to
leave the joiner's bench, or the wood-turning lathe,
to forego the pleasure of setting type or weaving cloth
on a handloom in order to write business letters, to
sum money columns, to supervise men's labour, to
attend board meetings, to bawl " quotations " through
a telephone, or smirk and tell lies to customers in a
warehouse !

With the modesty characteristic of present-day
writers I have in these papers refrained from directly
obtruding my personality! But my present theme
" lets me out," as Bret Harte's miner said. I am
constrained to be autobiographical. I have been
working as a printer, boy and man, for seventeen
years now, and have had plenty of time to get tired

of it; but I do say in all sincerity, in spite of the evil days upon which our noble craft has fallen, that had I to begin life over again, a printer I should be once more. Nay, were I to become a millionaire to-morrow, I should want to set up a little treadle machine or a handpress for myself, and, bringing together a stock of the finest types and the richest hand-made paper that money and taste could produce and procure, forget myself to realise myself in the production of such printing as William Morris alone has done as yet. When I had the printing-press going I should then want a carpenter's bench and a wood-turning lathe, from which I should want to turn out massive and, I hope, graceful and " spirited" "settles," and chairs, and tables, and bookcases for an admiring and grateful country-side. And the loom ! Ah, the loom would run the printing-press hard in its claim on my affections! What revelling in colour-com-binations ! What joy, when the warp was " beamed " and "twisted," to reach out for the traddles with my feet, for the lay with my left hand and the jigger-horn with my right, while the shuttles flew from end to end, and the shuttle-boxes clattered up and down for the changes of colour, and the web grew under my hands.

Where is the sense of all this multiplication of machines ? Here, for instance, is the linotype. Was not printing cheap enough—nay, was it not dirt cheap —before this demon came into the field ? There was no mechanical difficulty, standing in the way of public convenience, to call for its introduction, as was the case when the cylinder printing machine took the place of the hand-press, which could not turn out the news-sheets fast enough. There were plenty of compositors; the public and the advertisers were willing to pay. But now comes this automatic master, which does the work imperfectly, will probably always do it imperfectly, and which is operated by a man sitting cramped on a low stool, inhaling the fumes from the melting-pot, and monotonously dabbing a keyboard with his fingers all day or all night through. And there are young men in large numbers foolish enough to prefer this to hand-composition—an operation, even on plain book or news work, sufficiently pleasant and interesting to be a recreation to a *litterateur* and man of science like Peter Kropotkin. This linotype machine is ruining thousands of comps., it is flooding the country with trashy reprints, and it is doubtful if in the long run anybody will be a penny in pocket by it; for while the operator may get higher wages, his life will be shortened by the unhealthiness of the occupation.

It is just precisely in those directions where men should last think of introducing machines that they first think of introducing them. Domestic drudgery, cooking, washing, street-cleaning, mining—these are the matters to which a community not devil-driven would naturally wish mechanical contrivances to be applied; but because labour for those purposes is cheap there has been no great temptation to supersede the manual worker. But where there is a high standard of skill, and wages more or less to correspond, machinery may as soon as possible be expected to make its appearance.

I have heard young Socialists in Lancashire say
that they looked forward to a vast multiplication and
perfecting of machinery, enabling us to get along with
a working day of two or three hours. But of these
young friends I would ask : What will you do with
yourselves during the rest of the day ? Do you put
the little leisure you have even now to such good use
everywhere and always that you want so much more,
and that purchased, too, by your further degradation
during your working hours ? You will read, you say
(most excellent), and draw and paint (save the mark !),
and take photographs, and whip about in electrically-
propelled curricles (for cycling will be a means of
locomotion too simple and natural for you). Yes ;
and you will find the time hang heavily upon your
hands, and you will become a scandal-monger ; and
some of you will take to drink, if allowed ; and others
of you, if you are still full-blooded enough, will lead
astray the wife of another man who is leading a life as
vacuous and mischief-prompting as your own. But
no ; that would be too natural. You believe in getting
everything done by machinery : you will doubtless
get someone to invent an embracing machine. You
will become, if you are allowed, Kay Robinson's man
of the future, hairless and toothless, with one large
foot (the football foot), one large ear (the phonograph
or telephone ear), and one large hand (the lawn tennis
and type-writing hand). Seriously, my young friends,
when you come to realise what you want, and when
you know that what you want you can have, you will
prefer to do six hours' pleasant work per day rather
than three hours of work which is a weariness both to

body and mind. A society of men who are economically free, and who have awakened to a knowledge of the true aim of life, will refuse to allow machines to take from them any work which is worth doing and in the doing pleasant. Nature is not to be defrauded of her rights either in the things of the intellect or the things of the body. Suburban trains and tramcars would tempt us to ride ; but health demands that we should walk. Machinery takes manual labour from us ; and Nature has her revenge when she forces us to go and box and fence, and drearily swing and jump and lift weights in gymnasiums. The engineer looks forward to the time when the man with the muck rake can discard his rake and go and sit on the fence and watch a steam-digger or harvester go whirring round the field doing his work for him; but the man in the town longs for a garden in which to dig, and the medical scientist tells the scion of an effete stock that he had better get back to the soil.

In the society of the future men will revert to many of the simple and pleasant manual processes. There will be plenty of rough and dirty work in which no artistic pleasure can be taken, and for that machinery will be used to the fullest desirable extent. But while the Social-Democratic State will use machinery, it will refuse to be its slave. Society will be so impressed with the need of producing and developing the best men and women, physically and intellectually, that all conveniences, all satisfactions, and all " profits " will give way to this supreme convenience, this supreme satisfaction, this supreme profit. No more phossy jaw, no more potter's rot, no more lead poisoning, no

I

more wrist drop, no more specialisation and stultifica-
tion of a MAN into a maker of pin-heads!

With the obligation placed upon every capable man
and woman to bear his or her fair share of the world's
work, with the stoppage of the million wastes of competition, luxury, and warfare, with the savings effected
by a more co-operative style of living and working,
we shall have so much time on our hands that at first
we shall not know what to do with it; but the return
to simplicity in the processes of production will soon
suggest itself.   This is no mere sentimental fad of the
artists and literary men.   Men of such diverse tem-
peraments as William Morris the poet, and Peter
Kropotkin the savant, are agreed as to the necessity
of combining mental and physical labour, in the
interests of race-development and genuine progress in
the arts.   The claim for pleasure in their work will
come from the workmen themselves.

Reading, thinking, discussion, amusements, outdoor recreation, the cultivation of vocal and instru-
mental music, the discharge of one's duties as a parent
and a citizen—these will occupy much of the time of
the future man; but he will not want to follow all
these pursuits in his own person.   Few men have the
versatility to become, or to want to become, Admirable
Crichtons.   The normal man does not want to be an
indifferent amateur in half-a-dozen *dilettante* pursuits:
he prefers to be a sound professional in some one
pursuit.   He wants to have some one concern which
is the chief business of his life, his "work" properly
so-called.   He would not long tolerate a three hours
"day" of machine minding.   He will need his work

as he needs it-day. For, after all, the workman only fancies he does not want to work. Even if he is a reading man, the salt of literature loses its savour when he is out of a job, when he finds that he is living not in time, but in eternity, as Charles Lamb said when superannuated from the India House. As Zola urges again and again in the novel of "Dr. Pascal," from which the motto of this chapter is taken, work is the great law of healthy life. Through the food we eat, the beverages we drink, the air we breathe, we store up energy, and that energy must be dispensed again in work of hand and work of brain. When the worker is recovering from an illness he says: "I will not be right till I get back to my work again." He needs the physical exertion, the mental absorption and forgetfulness of self, the long fast between meals, and what a friend calls the peristaltic action, to keep body and mind in proper working order. Had Thomas Carlyle been a stone-mason like his stalwart, caustic-speaking, fighting fathers he never would have been the wretched dyspeptic he was.

The man of the future, using somewhat of his own taste instead of copying the work of bygone times when men were æsthetically free, putting sound materials into worthy work, and, as to the time required to do it well, no longer a slave to the market price, will hang over his work with something of the devotion of fabled Pygmalion. So that again we may see men realising themselves in an abandon of energy, a fever of diligence, such as that displayed by the masons who have carved those 8,000 statues on the cathedral of Milan, in many cases putting them away in obscure or distant niches where they will not be seen even from the cathedral roof! The citizens of the Social-Democratic State will be diligent, not from the ambition to "rise," not from outward compulsion, either of public opinion or dread of want, but from the intrinsic attraction of the labour itself, from the gracious inner compulsion of love and choice.

CHAPTER XIII.

PUBLIC SPIRIT.

" The objective social morality . . . becomes, when translated into a higher plane, the basis of the religion of Socialism, which consists in a sense of oneness with the social body ; in an identification of self-interest with social interest." – BAX.

" What is it that you would impart to me?
If it be aught toward the general good,
Set honour in one eye and death i' the other,
And I will look on both indifferently :
For let the gods so speed me as I love
The name of honour more than I fear death."
— SHAKESPEARE.

A JEW bidden to the wedding of a sister in the faith was required to contribute in kind towards the bride's wine cask. " What matters one flagon ? " said he as he poured a measure of water into the cask. The lady must have been unfortunate in her guests ; for, as the story goes, they had all reasoned after the same manner, and when the cask was broached it was found to contain water and naught else. To apply this as an exact analogue of the dearth of public spirit would be obviously unfair, for there is some public spirit whereas of wine there was none. But just as the dishonesty of each false contributor to the Semitic woman's wedding present came out in the result, so the lack of public spirit in the individual is made

manifest by the tardiness of general progress. By
flattery and entreaty each seeks to urge on his neighbour to make a stand for the general good, but
adventure our own fortunes we will not. With
profound confidence in our own ability to pilot and
compass great general changes, we are willing to put
forward for offices of risk and trial men whom we
lightly esteem. Our plea is that they can, as we
cannot, afford to make sacrifices; and that such honest
and plodding fellows are by their very lack of talent
(which we of course possess) cut out for danger,
drudgery, and the criticism of those they serve. Public
spirit is indeed rare and strange enough, and, as has
been indicated, the poverty of democratic achievement
is simply commensurate to the poverty of individual
performance.

Zeal for the common good is surely the crown and
flower of the virtues, and the absence of it in a man
ought to be one of the most shameful of the vices;
for as all profit by the general good, is it not the duty
of all to contribute to it? Obvious as the duty of
public service is, and beneficent as is the quality of
public spirit in its operation, there is no virtue held
in slighter regard, nor is there any vice to which men
will more readily confess than to the lack of public
spirit. Indeed the vice and the virtue are in this case
frequently transposed, activity in the public interest
being held in contempt, and selfish absorption in one's
own shop or family extolled as a high mark of personal
probity.

"'Ave you recorded your vote ?" asks Mr. Tozer,
the butter.nan, of Mr. Hopkins, the greengrocer, as

they look out from their adjoining shop doors on the evening of the election day. Mr. Tozer asks the question bashfully, as if he has a misgiving that the prosperous Hopkins will consider him frivolous.

" No I 'aven't," answers Hopkins severely, "and I don't mean to. I 'ave my business to attend to."

" You are quite right, Mr. Hopkins," chimes in Mrs. Tozer, who has joined her husband on the door step " Wot does it matter to uz 'oo gets in ? Folks in business 'ave no time to go runnin' after politics."

" Yes, there isn't much to choose between 'em," says Tozer hesitatingly.

He is not quite sure that even a shopkeeper should not take some interest in the Government of the country, and has actually asked Mrs. Tozer to let him go to the polling place. But his better half wants to keep right with both sides, and has a misgiving that if he records his vote it will become known that he voted for the Liberal, as he has indicated a desire to do. And the Liberal is a lawyer from London, with no local connection, whereas the Tory candidate is Mr. Parkyn, the brewer, who lives in the district —drives past the door to the brewery morning and afternoon, in fact—and has so many rich supporters in the neighbourhood, whose custom it would be so good to have with she and Tozer struggling to build up a business.

The cocksureness of Hopkins reassures Tozer that " Dosset " is his life concern, and he quiets his con- science by saying that there is not much to choose between them. He had an idea that if he voted for the Liberal and Local Control the vaults at the corner might be shut up, and that the women who can't pay their weekly bills would not make so many trips with the beer jug if they had to go a quarter of a mile lower down the street. But Hopkins has thriven, and Hopkins must be right.

" Saturday's a very awkward day for us to go and vote on," he says reflectively, as though wondering if he really could have managed it ; and then Hopkins changes the subject, and the butterman's conscience ceases from troubling.

As I have elsewhere put it :—" A business man may drink and fornicate, may play billiards, shoot pigeons, bet on racehorses, spend his time and money on a hundred and one useless or positively hurtful things, and his pursuits will be regarded as the legitimate recreation or, at worst, the excusable failing of a busy man. But let him dabble in politics, and his business friends will shortly begin to sneer and indulge in scornful head-tossings, and it will be generally agreed among them that it would better become him to attend to his business."*

Carriages and canvassers do not avail to bring out more than an insignificant proportion of the voters. Many Socialists, even, will not attend the meetings of their own trade union, where their hours of labour, wages, and other important matters are in large measure determined. Men who will pay money to stand and shiver in an east wind at a football match, or wade waist deep in a river for hours under the pretence of fishing, cannot be persuaded to listen to an hour's oratory at a street corner by the ablest

* " The Class War," pp. 6-7.

Socialist speaker; while many who pay money to tipsters, and every night eagerly scan the racing columns of sporting papers for "scratchings" and results, will be content to borrow week-old Socialist journals and dog-eared penny pamphlets. The suppression by law of beer and billiards in political clubs would be an interesting test of the genuineness of the Englishman's interest in public affairs. If one could imagine personal likes and dislikes, the law of social attraction and repulsion, no longer operating to send working men into the Socialist movement, how many of its present adherents would remain in it from sheer regard for the public policy? A goodly number, let me hasten to add; but would not the elimination of personal considerations make a considerable difference were such elimination possible as it is impossible?

The man who first declared that "everybody's business is nobody's business" surely did so regretfully, as does the ardent reformer who is to-day left to fight single-handed some hoary abuse defended by a strong vested interest. But one sometimes hears the proverb quoted triumphantly in defence of the lack of civic feeling, as if it were quite right that everybody's business *should* be nobody's business. The civic indifferentist adopts this reading because he is glad of any excuse for his neglect of the duties of citizenship, in the same way as a certain class of apologists for capitalism interpret the saying "The poor ye have always with you" to mean "The poor ye *shall* always have with you." The same feeling which prompts this attempt to excuse civic indifference renders the average man envious of one who comes

out from the ruck of his fellows as a public man.
" Who is he ? " the question is angrily asked, " that he
should take upon himself the *rôle* of guardian of the
public interest ? " And when an active trade unionist
gets victimised, the workmates who profit by his efforts
are not ashamed to say that " It does not do for a
man to make himself prominent in these matters."
The person engrossed in what Carlyle called " beaver-
ism" grudges that another should appear in a character
which he himself has neither inclination nor perhaps
ability to emulate ; and the feeling, perhaps vague
enough, of duty neglected, of trusts unworthily fulfilled,
lends rancour to the criticism.

When to the almost complete lack of civic ideals
we add the keenness of the struggle for existence, very
little more is required to account for the absence of
public spirit. The man in the street has not learned
to seek his own good in the general good. If his
position is to be improved he knows of no other way
of setting about it than by personal effort on self-
regarding lines. In the earlier days of the Socialist
movement in Aberdeen I once heard a worthy old
master blacksmith describe our branch meeting as an
assembly in which young men were taught " how to
get money without working for it"!—a most luminous
criticism from the enemy's point of view. The non-
Socialist citizen of the lower-middle and working
classes, having no idea of any very substantial benefits
to be gained through public channels, is not un-
naturally at a loss to account for the public spirit
displayed by a neighbour. His first supposition is
that there must be some axe to grind, some appoint-

ment to be obtained, some reward to be won as the
price of subsequent silence and subserviency. The
activity of one prominent Socialist has long ago been
explained by the allegation that he expected to be
bought over by the Government; but the price has
evidently not yet been paid, for the activity of the
gentleman in question is, if anything, increased rather
than diminished. He must be getting desperate. The
question so frequently put to the Socialist lecturer—
sometimes in mere friendly interest or curiosity—
" What do you get for all this ? " is an illustration of
the sheer inability to account for any species of active
work save on the motive of direct and immediate self-
interest.

If the man of public spirit is above the suspicion of
acting for money, and has notoriously refused prefer-
ment, the critics fall back on the naïve objection that
he is seeking popularity. By all that is base, we are
still at the stage when a man may without risk of
scathing reprobation avow his entire unconcern for
the public welfare, while at the same time let it be
suspected that another man is acting from that purest
of all self-regarding motives, the desire for the goodwill and approbation of his fellows, and with millions
of those who are profiting daily by the results of this
motive as it operated in the " named and nameless "
altruistic workers of times gone by, his case and
character will be settled out of hand. A woman will
pad her bust and hips and squeeze her waist so that
other women's husbands may admire and covet her;
a man will get his tailor to " improve " his shoulders
so that women shall, as he hopes, reckon him " a

fine man," and his fellow-mates dub him a "swagger chap"; or a wealthy Radical M.P. will buy a peerage, or a divine procure an American degree for £25 and a plagiarised treatise; and all these manifestations of the love of approbation in its more self-regarding form will be viewed with nothing beyond cynical amusement. But let some enthusiast spend the hours that ought to be devoted to sleep in writing letters to the papers regarding some undoubted public grievance to be abolished or benefit to be gained ; let him address meetings, buttonhole members of Parliament, or in one way or another put himself to a great deal of incon- venience in furtherance of the common good, and it will be considered that he is quite fairly told off, and his action effectually discounted, if it can be said : " He does it for popularity."

The best type of public worker is undoubtedly the one who is moved primarily by the desire for the public benefit aimed at, and only very secondarily, if at all, by considerations of how his efforts are likely to be regarded by his fellows. But the way of the reformer is so long, the hills are so numerous and so steep, and the roads are so bad, that as a rule he cannot afford to do without any legitimate crumbs of solace and encouragement offered on the journey ; and surely the desire for the approbation of our co- workers and our sympathisers present and prospective is a motive whose aid is altogether welcome so long as it is kept in its proper place. That is to say, so long as the individual does not subordinate that which is right to that which is merely likely to win approval.

Now, as has been pointed out in former chapters, it

is no very important concern of the New Ethic to look
to motives, since it adjudges acts virtuous or vicious
according as their results are social or anti-social. But
while there is no other safe and ultimate standard of
judgment by which to test the act when consummated,
men will always look to the motive that inspired the
act ; and one is glad to be able to say that the public
spirit which is prompted by the love of approbation is
the least egoistic of all the virtues, whether regard be
had to its motives or to its results. There can surely
be no motive less self-regarding than that which
depends for its gratification primarily on the gratification of others. The man who lays himself out to
make money, as a rule thinks primarily of himself, his
family, and at most his immediate friends. So far
from the general good having any place in his intellectual outlook, in many cases it would not be too
much to say that he will enjoy his comforts and
luxuries all the more from the knowledge that others
are precluded from similar enjoyments. Aristotle tells
us that men are more social than the ants and bees,
and Kropotkin would have us believe that "never at
any epoch, historical or geological, have individual
interests been in opposition to those of society." But
it is nevertheless true that there are people whose
enjoyment of a bright room and a good fire is enhanced
by seeing less fortunate mortals breasting the storm
without ; who are absolutely put into a better humour
by being able to look from their carriage windows on
others "plodding through the rain." This is human
nature in its *present* normal state ; but it is not the
human nature which makes for the love of approbation,

or which prompts men to spend themselves for the public good. It is quite enough for such persons that they approve of themselves. When his triumphs are wholly or partially won, the man of public spirit has his reward in viewing the benefits he has conferred and the esteem and gratitude of the people towards himself; but who shall say that this moral and intellectual gratification is to be put on all fours with the selfish pleasure of the money-maker when he increases his bank-balance by another figure? Philosophy may for analytical purposes find it necessary to bracket both species of motive together; but the lay judgment will always distinguish between the motive that prompts to giving and blessing and the motive that prompts to grasping and keeping. And the lay judgment is right.

Philosophers have landed themselves in endless confusion and controversy by the analysis of motives. It has been contended that we should cease to use the words egoism and altruism, since the so-called altruist, the self-sacrificing worker, derives as much satisfaction from his renunciation as the so-called egoist does from his aggrandisement. Bruno and Vanini surrender their lives rather than abjure what they believe to be the truth; and along comes the Utilitarian philosopher to prove that Bruno and Vanini had no choice; that they were so constituted mentally that to recant their doctrines would have caused them greater, because more protracted, suffering than was involved in the brief agony at the stake.

The analysing of motives in a case like this, however, proceeds from the desire to account for self-sacrifice in terms of the "happiness of the individual" who sacrifices himself. But, as Bax and Guyau both argue, the individual does not and cannot realise himself *in* himself. As Bax has it :—" The content, the meaning of individuality is not coincident with the form of the living individual or personality. Otherwise expressed, this content is not exhausted in its form, but seeks its completion outside its form. . It implies that the individual is, in other words, dependent—he is not a self-contained whole in himself, but merely an element in a larger whole." Or, as Guyau has it :— " We are not enough for ourselves; we have more tears than our sufferings claim, more capacity for joy than our own existence can justify." The man of highly socialised feeling has so many ties of sympathy, and the good opinion of friends and his own feeling of social duty done count for so much that, wanting these, life becomes a burden. The highest behest has to be complied with. Thus Bruno and Vanini may have been only humouring their consciences in offering themselves for martyrdom ; but are we for that reason to deny them the title of altruists? Are we to have no word to distinguish the act of him who sacrifices his life for the cause of truth and progress from the act of him who takes the lives of others to save his own or in pursuit of gain ? The New Ethic adjudges acts altruistic and egoistic, not according to motives, but according to results. If your act is primarily for yourself it is egoistic. If, on the contrary, it is primarily for the public good it is altruistic. We cannot afford to lose terms that add to the resourcefulness of the language.

Christianity, with its central idea of personal "salvation" as the great aim of life, has undoubtedly done
much to retard the growth of Public Spirit. Jesus
himself gave no indication that he had any conception
of the corporate character of society. He was either
careless about the matter or was fairly well satisfied
with the then existing political and economical forms.
His idea would appear to have been that the one
thing needful to a perfect social aggregate was to have
perfect social units, overlooking the fact that a body is
more than its members, as a building is more than a
heap of bricks and stones and timber, and that, with
inequitable societary institutions and no organisation
of social processes, selfishness must remain a necessity
of self-preservation, and individual perfection be a
distant and forever unattainable ideal. The message
of Jesus was altogether to the individual as a person
having a soul to be saved, not to the citizen as having
social duties to perform and civic machinery to perfect.
In the domain of politics he practised what Renan
calls "the doctrine of transcendent disdain." His
kingdom was not of this world. And apart from the
non-civic character of the teaching of Jesus himself,
the fact that his earlier followers lived in daily ex-
pectation of the Second Coming and the Crack of
Doom would naturally disincline them to trouble
much as to social changes. This posture of civic subserviency would be intensified by the comparatively
helpless position in which they found themselves as
a fraction of a subject people, living under the all-
powerful empire of the Cæsars. The instructions as
to social arrangements given by Paul in his Epistles

recognise the necessity for certain forms of corporate organisation ; but they are instructions for the order-ing of simple homogeneous religious communities rather than forms suitable to a great and complex community, not held together by any uniform religious bond. They have not the appearance of being in-tended for any wide secular and civic application. In spite of the attempts to import into the teaching of Jesus a vast deal of politico-economical significance, it seems tolerably certain that the Master was no politician. He appears, in fact, to have belonged to that school of " social " philosophers whose creed has been aptly described by Huxley as Administrative Nihilism ; and the state of neglect into which all affairs, and especially all public affairs, fell towards the end of the tenth century, when the Crack of Doom was once again expected, was simply the reduction to its logical absurdity of his principle of " transcendent disdain " for temporal concerns.

The school of Administrative Nihilists has now many adherents who have in most respects little in common with the founder of Christianity. Henry Thomas Buckle, Herbert Spencer, Peter Kropotkin, and Auberon Herbert would scarcely be claimed by any of the Christian sects ; but they show the true Christian scorn of the " temporal power " and all its works." With them the principle of " transcendent disdain " becomes a principle of raging hostility, in which the State is attacked with something approach-ing to Apostolic fervour. To them the State would appear to be typified in the tax-gatherer. The classes to which they belong, and whose standpoint they have

K

adopted in its most exaggerated form, have obtained
about as much from the Legislature as they expect to
get. The Legislature, acting through the Executive,
will protect their persons and property, will help
them to enforce their contracts, will guard their
blacklegs, will inspect their houses and drains, their
food and drugs; and that is about all they wish
it to do. When it passes on to make the employer
liable for preventible accidents, when it compels him
to provide a certain number of cubic feet of air space
in the workshop or factory, to fence his machinery,
to ventilate his mines, and to have his ladders,
scaffoldings, and boilers inspected, and when, finally,
it begins to take the business of production and dis-
tribution out of his hands altogether, he and his
spokesmen immediately cry out: "Not too much
Government, but just Government enough"! Their
idea of the functions of the State is, as Lassalle said
long ago, "a night watchman's idea." The great
body of mankind have for centuries viewed society as
a concourse of independent human atoms, bound to
spend their lives in never-ending strife with one
another, with Government to do nothing beyond
looking on and "keeping the ring" for the social
"mill." With such a conception of society and of
the function of Government what wonder is it that
the social instinct common to all mankind should
have experienced so much difficulty in translating
itself into public spirit ?

One may excuse the anti-statist diatribes of a critic
like Burke, who lived in a century when the functions
of Government were mainly repressive, when

vexatiously restricted the citizen instead of bene-
ficently serving him. Similarly we may account for
the Anarchism of Kropotkin, who, as a Russian,
knows the State chiefly as an organised system of
robbery and despotism ; though even Kropotkin might
by this time have learned to distinguish between the
use of Government and the abuse of it. But there is
less excuse for the one-sided political philosophy of
the historian Buckle, and absolutely no excuse for
the hopeless perversity of Herbert Spencer. In a
passage which the Anarchists are fond of quoting,
Buckle says :

Every great reform which has been effected has consisted, not
in doing something new, but in undoing something old. The
most valuable additions made to legislation have been enact-
ments destructive of preceding legislation; and the best laws
which have been passed have been those by which some former
laws were repealed.

This untenable thesis is based solely on such
measures as the Catholic Emancipation Act, the Act
removing the Civil Disabilities of the Jews, with,
above all, the Acts repealing the Corn Laws. It
would be nearer the truth to say that the best legislation has been that which created rights and privi-
leges to the whole people as against classes and
individuals holding power and enjoying possession,
not with the assistance of the law, but by means of
superior force and superior cunning. Legislation did
not establish slavery and serfdom ; but it abolished
them in some States and it helped to abolish them in
all. Magna Charta gave rights which no previous law
or charter either denied or affirmed. So did the Bill
of Rights, so did the Factory Acts. The Reform Bills

of '32 and '67 and '85 did not so much abolish previous legislation as create additional civic rights and powers for the whole people. The Municipal Corporations Act of 1835, the Merchant Shipping Acts, Mines Regulation Acts, Truck Act, Education and Free Libraries Acts did not abolish previous legislation, but called into existence new legal rights to remove old social wrongs. The evils from which civilised nations suffer to-day are not evils which have been directly created by law. They are rather evils which have arisen because there was no law and no practice to prevent them from arising.

The first volume of the " History of Civilisation," which contains Buckle's famous pronouncements on legislation, appeared in 1857, while Spencer has been the champion of Individualism from about 1860* up to the present time. Now, during this period of practically forty years Government has been passing more and more out of the repressive and entering more and more upon the administrative stage; and the precise abuses of government which, 100 years ago, excused Burke's attacks upon the institution of Government itself no longer exist to justify the attacks made on it by modern Administrative Nihilists. To be sure, Government is still to too great an extent negative, prohibitive, and punitive rather than constructive, administrative, and beneficent. But the State, with all its defects, has done more for every one of us than any one of us has done for

* In the *Westminster Review* for April, 1860, appeared his first anti-Socialistic article, " Parliamentary Reform : the Dangers and the Safeguards."

the State ; and one might be pardoned for expecting
that historians and philosophers, writing in the later
decades of the nineteenth century, would have realised
somewhat of the necessity and utility of the vast
administrative activity upon which the State and the
municipalities are entering. What all these critics of
Government overlook is the fact that the political
machinery has been proved most effective for the
classes who have in turn controlled it, and that if the
Democracy make as good use of its political power
as the Aristocracy did prior to 1832, and as the
Plutocracy has done since, it may achieve greater
results for itself than even these orders have achieved
for themselves. It is no part of our business to
discuss here the case for Social-Democracy as against
Anarchy. Suffice it to say that the followers of
Herbert Spencer and Michael Bakounine entirely
misread the necessities and tendencies of the times
when they ask us to leave in the hands of the present
governing classes an institution which, whether to
make or to prevent social change, is the strongest
weapon at the command of the democracy.

From such depressing views of the State and its
functions it is refreshing to pass to such social
philosophy as is contained in the following passage
from Laurence Gronlund :

It is society, organised Society, the State, that gives us all
the rights we have. To the State we owe our freedom. To it
we owe our living and property, for outside of organised Society
man's needs far surpass his means. The humble beggar owes
much to the State, but the haughty millionaire far more ; for
outside of it they both would be worse off than the beggar now
is. To it we owe all that we are and all that we have. To it

we owe our civilisation. It is by its help that we have reached
such a condition as man individually never would have been
able to attain. Progress is the struggle with Nature for mastery,
is war with misery and inabilities of our "natural" condition.
The State is the organic union of us all to wage that war, to
subdue Nature, to redress natural defects and inequalities. The
State, therefore, so far from being a burden to the "good," a
"necessary evil," is man's greatest good.

Those words reflect something like the spirit shown
by the pagans of the great classical Republics in their
attitude towards the State and the public good. It
would be idle to pretend that the slaveholding democ-
racies of Greece and Rome represent a Golden Age
of public spirit, in which there was no alloy of self-
seeking and corruption on the part of either individuals
or classes. But a very superficial study of Greek and
Roman life and institutions is sufficient to show that
regard for the public good carried men to lengths of
daring and self-sacrifice far exceeding anything in the
history of modern (including mediæval) times.

Making due allowance for the legendary character
of much that comes to us as Greek and Roman
history, what is there in the literature of Christian
civilisation to compare with the stories of the Brutuses
(first and last), of Scævola, of Horatius Cocles, of
Leonidas and the Three Hundred, of the voluntary
martyrdom of Marcus Curtius, of those brilliant and
unfortunate brothers, the Gracchi, or of the implacable
Regulus, who, even for the prayers and tears of his
fellow-citizens, refused to save himself from torture
and death when the price of his life meant a temporary abatement of the advantage of his country?
Granted that they were men of blood and iron; that

they were accustomed to the spectacle of death and the thoughts it suggested ; that the conditions of the times were entirely different from those of our day. When all allowances have been made, it is clear that the standard of public spirit and the love of country and fellow-citizens must have been infinitely superior to anything that the modern community can produce.

But when we come to study the social polity and habits of life of the Romans in particular we cease to wonder that public spirit should reach so high a standard. With their simple, sociable, leisurely open-air life ; their games, chariot-races, religious processions and military triumphs ; the frequent meetings of the gentes or houses for their common sacrifices ; the assemblage of the patricians in the senate and comitia curiata, of the plebeians in their tribes, and of the whole people in their comitia centuriata, the people of Rome could scarcely fail to be welded together with something of the community of sympathies and fellow-feeling that obtains in a model household. These gatherings were always held with some definite object in view ; and the leisure of the freeman would permit of questions of public policy and procedure being fully discussed, with frequent reference, doubtless, to broad general principles of statecraft. Among a people thrown so much together, in such circumstances, public opinion would be a force more strongly opera-tive than even to-day, with our all-discovering and all-revealing newspaper press ; while they would possess a power of concerted and enthusiastic action which modern men, with their segregated and anti-social way of living and working, cannot even realise, far less emulate.

Much of all this refers to Greece as well as to Rome; but in Greece there was in addition the strong social bond supplied by the romantic comradeships which existed among the young men, and which went far to make the Greek phalanx so formidable in war, and to knit together the men of the country in the pursuits of peace; for those romantic attachments long outlived the period of youth and bachelorhood, and doubtless helped to soften the asperities of debate and to promote unity in public policy. To those who so freely gave their lives to the State the renunciation of property would come easy; and it was a common practice with wealthy citizens to hasten to hand over to the civic authorities works of art of which they happened to become possessed. This did not mean that they gave of their superfluities, after the manner of a Carnegie or Rylands to-day. The principle rather was that the very finest works of art were too valuable to be monopolised by individuals. A principle which will apply, and happily in some measure always has applied, to the giving of much besides statuary and paintings.

It is, indeed, admitted on every hand that in the early and the climacteric periods of Greek and Roman development of all the virtues took a manly and civic turn, as different as possible from the ascetically-morbid and selfishly-introspective Christian "morality" which succeeded it.

To indicate how public spirit was created and maintained in the classical republics is to afford some idea of how it may be created and maintained in the Social-Democratic State. First of all, the intellectual revolution has to be brought about. The feeling of hostility to the State and distrust of it as such must be removed. The Irishman who, on landing in New York, declared himself "agin" the Government, whichever Government it was, represents an insurrectionary spirit not by any means confined to the natives of the Green Isle. The modern man is always more or less opposed to the constituted authorities even if it be only the committee of his trade union. Public opinion is wholly in favour of the "besting" of men in uniform. Have we not all seen at one time or another a policeman and a burly ruffian roll over one another in the street, with respectable people looking on, and no one offering to help "the under dog" as represented by the policeman? Socialists are never so popular as when in conflict with the "law'norder" for which the people are themselves responsible.

But with the multiplication of public parks, baths, libraries, and reading rooms, municipal trams, lodging-houses, and public houses,* the worker should ere long begin to see that the public authorities are not there merely to draw their wages for taxing him and keeping him down. As he realises the advantage of public enterprise he will come to believe in making the authorities his servants instead of leaving them his masters, against whose official power he vainly kicks so long as he neglects to use his civic power to control and direct them. Earning his living in the service of some department of the State or some committee of

---

* There is only the one at Elan Village, Birmingham, as yet; but that has been so successful that it will soon be necessary to speak of them in the plural number.

the Town Council, he will more and more recognise
the necessity of putting his friends, rather than his
enemies, on the board of directors that employs him.
In the course of attending to his own interests he will
come naturally to take an interest in all departments
of public business.   He will at length find politics as
interesting as billiards or football.

The social and civic instincts will be developed in
the man of the future in much the same way as they
were developed in the men of the Greek and Roman
cities.   With greatly increased leisure, frequent
holidays, and the means as well as the opportunities
of rational social enjoyment, men and women will be
brought together much oftener, and will meet under
the most favourable circumstances.   The diffusion
among the people of knowledge and ideas will give
them materials for conversation somewhat more entertaining than the three staple elements of "shop,"
scandal, and what they had for dinner.   The county
families attend race meetings and cricket matches, not
so much to see the races or the cricket as to meet one
another and to spend the day in the open air.   From
much of all this Demos is to-day shut out.   But
in the Social-Democratic State he will be able to
attend the games, regattas, and races, the laying of
foundation stones and the opening of public buildings;
and, feeling himself freeman and social equal with
any there—"one of the owners" as the Paisley weaver
described himself to the admiral of the Channel Fleet
—he will recognise that he has his part and his interest
in all that goes on for the good of the civitas.   The

religion of the average man is himself; but set him free from the fear of want and the anxiety after money, and he will make a religion of his work and his civism; for it is incredible that he should go back again to any form of theological superstition. And just as on election day now the aristocrat puts favours on his coachman's whip and goes forth with his wife and daughters to bring in voters for the maintenance of monopoly and class privilege —carefully disinfecting his carriage after- wards—so the free citizens of the future will be up and doing in the interests of the common good, not merely on one day, but every day and all the day, in private as in public life.

> " Ah, such are the days that shall be !
> But what are the deeds of to-day,
> In the days of the years we dwell in,
> That wear our lives away ? "

Life must always in the main consist of the private and personal business of hewing wood and drawing water, of building and planting, and the pursuits of seedtime and harvest. But while we must keep firm hold on the private and domestic virtues, we must at all times be prepared to go to barricades of one sort or another *pour la solidarité humaine.* And, as public spirit is still so rare among mankind, it is correspond- ingly valuable where it is to be found. As the world grows older the ape and tiger die out in men, and the revolutionist, the man of public spirit, is no longer openly baited to death as were the Brunos and Vaninis of byegone days. Nor, with the death of superstition in its grosser forms, is he called upon to emulate the sacrifice of that devoted Roman who, clad

in full armour, lept between the jaws of the earth-
quake for his city's sake. But if the conditions of
martyrdom change, the spirit of consecration to the
public good is more needful than ever. The cross of
hard work has still to he borne, and the stake of
suffering to be faced. The old-time martyr served his
cause by dying for it. The modern martyr must be
content to serve his cause by living and working for
it—

> " Unknown, if not maligned,
> Forlorn, forlorn, bearing the scorn
> Of the meanest of mankind."

And when his work is done he may well leap into a
gulf which gives back no immortality of fame such as
attended the last leap of Marcus Curtius. But there
are consolations by the way ; and if a man look not
ever down he will often see light ahead.

CHAPTER XIV.

PRESENT POSSIBILITIES OF MORAL IMPROVEMENT.

"Ideals are mighty, though for the most part held and acted on unconsciously. But it is they who scrutinise and appraise ideals—who have distinct conceptions of what is valuable in life—it is they who sway the minds of the throng of hasty wayfarers. Let us be fully persuaded in our own minds. If we are, and if we hold and prize our ideal, depend upon it we shall act upon it, and get others to act upon it. If our cherished ideal of life contradicts and excludes evil tendencies in thought or action our ways of life will do so too ; and social and pleasant ways of life are contagious. . . . Ideals are not only for the life to come—they are the salvation of the life that now is when they are held in the noble and steadfast mind."—THEO. CHAPMAN.

WE sometimes hear Socialists arguing that, without great industrial and economic changes, it is impossible to diffuse education and refinement among the people. By this they must mean *ideal* education and *perfect* refinement, since the people have some of both already and are daily acquiring more.

In "Anarchist Morality" we have Kropotkin main-taining, in effect, that the teaching of morality is of no use ; that the morality of a period is the necessary expression of its economic conditions ; and that the altered conditions of life of the future will in them-selves produce men who cannot help being moral because of the excess of their social feeling. But our

Anarchist friend here confounds the practice of morality with the knowledge of what morality requires. The man of the future cannot be left to his mere intuitions of what is or is not moral. It is surely of some advantage to know what is and what is not right conduct, and to bring all the arts of logical demonstration and persuasive exhortation to bear for the enforcement of the moral sanction. One of the most efficient correctives to bad and encouragements to good conduct is the critical influence of a healthy public opinion; but how is the compulsion of a healthy public opinion to be brought to bear upon conduct if there is to be no declared standard of morality? if everybody is to be left to decide for himself what is right and what wrong. The community which possessed no ethical ideal, which in the domain of conduct proceeded throughout on the assumption that whatever is is right because it is the necessary expression of the economic conditions—this would indeed be a hopelessly immoral aggregation of human beings. Happily, such a community never has existed and never will exist.

On all fours with the view of Kropotkin is the *ad captandum* conclusion of Bernard Shaw (as arrived at in that clever book "The Quintessence of Ibsenism"), that the individual does what he wants to do and finds the reason and justification of it afterwards. It is surely altogether preposterous, however, to argue as if considerations of right and wrong did not determine what the individual should do and what he should avoid. Bad as things may be, we are neither so foolish nor so hoggishly unsocial as this would amount to.

We venture to say that Mr. Bernard Shaw, bent as
he professes to be on mere self-realisation, is every
day doing things as a matter of duty and good citizenship which he does not by any means wish to do.

There is, of course, much truth in the view that the
average morality of a period is the expression of the
economic conditions then obtaining. But the doctrine
of averages is about as misleading in morals as it is in
the statistics of the apologists of capitalism. Because
the worker with 25s. a week receives the present
statistical average, for the worker, of £64 a year, that
is no reason why he should conclude that under the
present system he cannot better his position ; nor
need we be satisfied with the average morality of the
period if, by increasing the number of those whose
morality is above the average, we can raise the
average itself. Even the average man passes his life
in a more or less vehement protest, by action if not by
speech, against the economic conditions ; and the most
tyrannical and grasping landlord or capitalist is not in
every respect as bad as the law of the land and the
sanctions of political economy would allow him to be.
The world-wide existence of a great and growing
Socialist movement, which has everywhere derived its
light and leading from men who have "put by ease
and rest" for the attainment of an ideal they can
hardly hope to realise with any degree of fulness in
their lifetime—this alone affords ample proof that
ethically we are not under the absolute domination of
the economic conditions.

Instead of being so entirely the slaves of our economic environment, there is good reason to believe

that unjust social conditions are due to the moral and
intellectual apathy of the people, to a state of mind
and character which must be altered by instruction
and exhortation before the economic conditions can be
improved. It is just possible to emphasise too strongly
the partial truth that man is the creature of circumstances. There is a danger of too readily falling in
with the tendency to excuse the individual for what
may be preventible failings by putting the blame on
the conditions. The individual may, as a rule, be
safely left to find excuses for himself. While holding
fast to charity in judging the offender after the offence
is committed, there must be no fatalism before the fact
— no foregone conclusion by the individual or by
others that he is obliged to do what he feels tempted
to do. There is a danger of reading into the biological
theories as to the influence of environment and heredity
a species of predestination which is more insidious than
the old Calvinistic doctrine known by that name.
The theological doctrine referred to the world to come,
and as the individual could not know till the day of
judgment what fate had been foreordained for him, he
could not anticipate it ; but the scientific doctrine
refers to this life, and a too rigorous application of it
would mean that we should regard all existing evil
tendencies as inevitable simply because they were
there. To do this is to overlook the part played by
the individual moral consciousness and by public
opinion in modifying hereditary tendencies, as well as
by the modifications effected by the individual on his
own immediate environment, and their reaction on
him.

Not only have men collectively the power to alter their circumstances, but much may be done by the individual in his personal and non-civic capacity towards improving the immediate conditions of his life. We are not, all of us, making the most of the opportunities which even a defective social system affords us for mental and moral development and for social service. We are mostly good citizens in the sense that we take a keen interest and an active part in important public affairs. In fact, as a party we have no equals in active and intelligent citizenship. But the duties of citizenship, important as they are, form only one branch of the whole duty of man, and I am sometimes inclined to think that some of us are so much occupied with public business that we rather neglect our own private business. By "private business" I do not mean merely pecuniary or other similar prudential concerns. I am anxious to set up a high personal standard for Socialists. I want to be able to believe, with the least possible misgiving, that it is the best men and women, morally and intellectually, who find their way into the Socialist movement. The outside public rightly judge a cause by the sort of people it attracts or produces; and it would be an immense comfort for one to be able to say to the hostile or indifferent spectator: " We have in this movement the best workmen, the best husbands, fathers, friends, and neighbours—the best all-round good fellows in every respect. Your social arrangements do not give us the opportunities we think we ought to have; but we ask no indulgence on that ground. We protest against your system, but we

L

make the best of it. It is true we do not amass money; we have only one life to live, and have something better to do with our time than devote it to the dreary and anti-social frivolity in which your Barnatos and Vanderbilts spend their brief and ignoble careers. But in such matters as knowledge, skill, taste, power of speech, literary ability, capacity and zeal for useful work, orderliness of life and conversation, kindliness, honesty, charity, generosity, sociability—in all these we shall as a party take second place to no body of men in the same station of life."

That is the claim I should like to be able to make on behalf of the Socialists as a party. Even if we are "as good as our neighbours" in the ordinary habits and practices of life, that is not enough for me. I want to see Socialism making its adherents quite obviously and unmistakably better men and better women than those who are still without the gate. I want the name of Socialist to be a hall-mark, a generally recognised and accepted guarantee of ability, integrity, and lovableness. We are asking the people to recast their habits of thought, to discard the individualistic ideal of rising on the shoulders of our fellows, of succeeding by the failure of others— the hope and desire of which for ourselves and the admiration of which in others go so far to reconcile alert natures to the present system—and we must show our better ideal working out to finer issues in our own conduct and character.

In most workshops there is some man who serves as a kind of model and leader among his workmates.

Men come to him with their troubles and their confidences; they consult his experience when in difficulty; they crack his jokes over again ; they quote him as an authority ; they copy even his tricks of speech and style of dress.   Now, in factory and workshop, in field and mine, in office and warehouse, or wherever men are gathered together I want this man who is noted for sympathy and sagacity to be the Socialist, and I want him to be worthy of the respect accorded to him. When a man is known to be churlish or stingy, a duffer as a workman, or a money-lender extracting interest for petty loans, to be cruel to, or careless of, his wife and children, to have scores standing against him at a number of beerhouses round about, or to be in debt to several men in the place—when a man is chargeable with a number of these things, what an amount of discredit he throws upon any good cause with which he may be connected.   His principles will be tried, not upon their merits, but upon his demerits. That they are the principles of such an ill-conditioned fellow will be enough to condemn them.   Whereas the principles of the former type of man will have as much adventitious advantage with his fellows as those of the other will have perhaps undeserved opprobrium. Therefore I say that it is of the utmost importance that we should, in spite of all difficulties, cultivate those qualities of mind and body, of conduct and character, which, while good in themselves and in their immediate results, redound to the credit of the general social ideal by which our lives are regulated.

I have written these chapters, not in the spirit of the superior person who fancies that from a mental

or moral coign of vantage he can look down upon, and
speak down to, the common and erring mortals who
form the ruck of humanity. Rather I want us to take
counsel together, to see wherein we are lacking, and,
by deciding and declaring together publicly that
certain matters of being and doing should be otherwise than as they are or have been, perhaps we shall
be able, by the common stand we make, to help one
another to act up, as individuals, to the high and
exacting standard which is surely required by a social
ideal such as ours. I take my share—the share of a
worker in the ranks—of any blame I may appear to
be dispensing over the movement as a whole.

Referring cursorily to the subject of ethics, a writer
in a Socialist weekly declared some time ago that
"present-day morality is good enough for us," present-
day morality being, he said, "the necessary corollary
of present economic conditions." But, I would ask,
whose "present-day" morality is it that is good enough
for us? The morality of Jack-the-Ripper or the morality
of Father Damien? the morality of the procuress or
that of the sister of mercy? the morality of greedy Jay
Gould or of that man of renouncements Leo Tolstoi?
These are (or were) contemporaries; but how different
their morals!

Or take the details of two concrete cases which will
appeal more closely to those to whom I mainly address
these chapters. Here are two workmen subject in
every way to the same economic conditions. Working
the same hours, at the same trade, in the same shop,
and for the same wages, their morals are yet as dis-
similar as possible. One, a Socialist, has a decent

home in a comparatively open, sunny, working-class street, five minutes' walk from the park and the open country. His wife and children are cleanly and comfortably clad; he has a piano for his girls; he has a few hundred books in his little parlour; his children are growing up; but he is anxious to keep them at school as long as he can. The major part of his leisure time he devotes to reading, writing, attending public meetings, and the meetings of his trade union. On Sunday mornings he goes off reluctantly from his books and his bairns to some neighbouring town to lecture on Socialism. It is not work he is specially fond of; though sometimes when thoroughly warmed to his theme he does really enjoy speaking. Though not naturally cut out for oratory, and having little or no ambition that way, he feels that the work has to be done, and, in the absence of a sufficiency of better and wiser speakers, he is willing to do even more than his fair share of it. Though the having to overcome his constitutional nervousness and self-consciousness and speak in public sometimes seems the great burden of his life, it is a burden he elects to bear. He makes his career one long renunciation of his chiefest pleasures. With a strong, a life-long hankering after the pleasant byeways of mere literature (he became a Socialist through book study), his reading, his attendance at all sorts of meetings, his goings out and his comings in are all made subordinate and contributory to the furtherance of a great social ideal. Even at his work he toils harder and more steadily than those who, in the employer's eyes, have no bar sinister of militant social heresy to help them to dismissal. This is the

propagandist, the man of duty; and those who know
the movement know that it contains many such men.
But his workmate, subject, as has been said, to the
same economic conditions, is a man of pleasure, or at
any rate of indulgence, for his pleasures are of that
gross and selfish kind which frequently defeat the
purpose of the pleasure-seeker. Spending a third of
his week's wages in drink, and frequently "losing
time," he "retrenches" by living in a shabby back
street, and he effects a further "saving" in the matter
of dinners by having none except on Sunday. On
Mondays the family have the remains of Sunday's
dinner cold, and on Tuesday, if Saturday's pay is not
entirely spent, the mid-day meal may consist of potato
pie; but on most days of the week his wife and children
will have to make bone and blood and tissue as best
they can with bread and butter, tea, coffee, or beer.
As to his social duties, when asked if he means to
attend a meeting of his trade union, he scornfully
queries, with some sort of idea that it excuses his
non-attendance, "Oh, what'll *they* do?" or he will
object "Why don't they" do this or that? as though
"they" were some sort of outside agency over which
he had no control and for which he had no responsibility. In politics, unless he has made bets on the
election, he swells the list of those who "did not vote."
Saturday afternoon is spent in a public house, to
which his wife comes for as much of his money as she
can rescue. Well on in the evening the couple go
out to "buy in" beef and greens for the event of the
Englishman's week, leaving the elder children at home
to pluck the younger ones out of the fire and keep

them, if possible, from overturning the lamp; for of course there is no gas in the house. On the way to the noisy street where the butchers' and greengrocers' shops abound, the husband and wife call at the Hen and Chickens, where the concert and the beer detain them till closing time; and *then* the marketing has to be done, the butcher having to keep open till long past midnight to suit their convenience.

Next day the propagandist has to leave behind him his own cool and pleasant parlour, and will eat the eternal beef and potatoes in some fellow workman's kitchen, which, although it opens straight to the street, is stifling hot and full of the smell of burning fat. But our man "as looks after hisself" stays at home, and, putting in the day with a Sunday paper and a beer can, goes to bed with his stomach full of ale and his brain in a hopeless muddle, just as the propagandist is making his way home after a hard and perhaps fruitful day's work. On Monday morning the latter will be tired, and will regret that there is no Sabbath for him. But the man of self-indulgence will be still more tired. He will have an aching head, a face redder and more blotchy than ever, and he will have a diuretic attack as the punishment of his week-end gorging and swilling.

These are not merely types; they are portraits. Not merely lay figures on which I have hung, the virtues on the one, the vices on the other, but living men whom I know. The propagandist is not all self-sacrifice and consideration for others. He is, in fact, a bit opinionated and inclined to bully those who cannot argue yet will not be persuaded; and his very ardour frequently makes him a bad loser when he gets beaten in small things. Neither is the man of self-indulgence devoid of good qualities. He sings a good song, is a cheerful and waggish companion, and is willing to "get his hand down" when a friend is in the straits he has often been in himself. But the one is living a life of strenuous manhood and active citizenship, and will not only leave the world better than he found it, but will leave healthy and intelligent children to inhabit and still further improve it; the other is a good-natured hog, happy with his swill, and hoping rather than working for the best to himself and all mankind. His children will in all probability live the lives of their parents over again.

Now, the economic conditions do not seem to be exactly all-powerful here. For all the similarity there is in the habits, thoughts, and general mode of life of the two men they might well belong to different classes, different races, or different centuries. Who will say that we cannot, even under the conditions of Individualism, increase the number of the one class and vastly diminish that of the other? Who will say that we cannot, by precept, example, and missionary institutions of a social as distinguished from a religious character, help to civilise the self-indulgent barbarians, transforming them in increasing numbers into really respectable men and women and useful citizens.

It may be said that the fact that we do not do so is reason good for supposing that the thing cannot be done. But, I ask, have we as Socialists ever tried? Have we made any attempt to do in a general way what Toynbee Hall in London and the Ancoats

Brotherhood in Manchester have attempted to do in a local and partial way ? Of course we have not, and small blame to us, since we have been so busy with the propaganda of social change as distinguished from personal reform. Our lecturers have gone down into the dark places of Christian barbarism, and they have spoken to the people of the Iron Law of Wages, of theories of value, and of the necessity for independent Socialist action in politics, and at the same time we have denounced Thrift,* and told men, already too contented with their position, that individually and apart from political action they had no power to better it. All this has been rightly put in evidence, and must be kept in evidence for yet many a day ; but does it represent the whole of our message to man, or is it not necessary that something further in the nature of a philosophy of life should be put before those who are already satisfied with our public policy ? Are those who have been attending our meetings all these years never to hear anything beyond expositions of our more elementary social and economic doctrines ? We forget that the majority of those present at indoor meetings are at one with us on most of the subjects we discuss, and that much of what we tell them of economics and politics they have already read in books, pamphlets, and newspapers. The consequence of this continual hearing of lectures on co operation, elementary Socialism, trade unionism, and politics is that when a

* This is a much abused word. In Socialist criticism it is usually employed as meaning *saving*, whereas more properly it means good husbandry, carefulness in expenditure and consumption, not the withholding from use or consumption altogether.

man has attended Socialist meetings for a year or two he begins to lose his interest in propaganda. If he continues to attend the meetings he does so more as a matter of duty, and "to encourage the others," than because of the pleasure or benefit he derives; for he has the feeling that he rarely hears anything new. In all our largest branch organisations, if they have been in active propagandist existence for a few years, the majority of the members are quite indifferent about propaganda. If they go to the club premises at all they have to be hunted out of the ante-rooms and from the bar and play tables when the lecture is about to commence. This is no doubt due in some measure to the ineffectiveness of many of the speakers; but the mere iteration of certain phrases and ideas, and the limited scope of our propaganda, have to do, much more than anything else, with the failure of the average man to keep up a steady interest in the intellectual part of our work.

For my part, I have never been content to regard cur organisations as missionary centres with a floating membership, institutions kept going so that men may attend for a few years, and, having picked up a few ideas regarding Socialism as a public movement, gradually drift away from us, satisfied that they have learned all we have to teach. One likes to think of the Socialist meeting-place as a centre of light and leading for the working class on all the great concerns of life; and I am sure all the best men among us want to see our adherents growing year by year in knowledge and in understanding, stimulated to study and to think on their own account by what they hear at the meetings from week to week. As it is, the written lecture is tabooed; the speaker must deal with some plain and simple subject on which he can without difficulty speak extemporaneously; and any excursion into the field of history, general literature, physical science, or art criticism, if not exactly forbidden, is regarded as something very manifestly apart from the purposes of the organisation.

Let our candidates for public office and our propagandists out of doors be as plain and practical as possible. Let them stick to politics, economics, and sociology as closely as may be. But while we remember that our primary duty is a public duty, and pay all due attention to our definite public policy, let us at the same time remember that we have an intellectual duty to ourselves—the duty, namely, of teaching one another the best we know on all the important personal concerns of life. We know and can conceive of nothing beyond Nature and man, and have simply "no pockets" for anything referring to God and a future life; yet, while having no wish to invent or suggest any new religion, we may still be of opinion that man lives not by politico-economical bread alone.

Many ardent Socialists will dissent from any project or even suggestion of moral improvement under existing social conditions. Their view will be that considerations of personal character must wholly give way to the supreme concern of advancing those social changes which we speak of in bulk as the Social Revolution. According to this view, I suppose it matters not whether a propagandist pay his milkman or not provided he is a good and a willing speaker; and, similarly,

I take it, Jack Wragge may get drunk and rouse the
street on Saturday night, and his sin will be forgiven
him if he turn up to sell *Justice* and " The Moral
Effects of Socialism " at the Sunday-morning meeting.
Experience of what has actually happened justifies me
in saying that this is not putting the matter in an
extreme or unwarrantable form ; and so put, I submit
that the theory that character and Socialism have
nothing to do with one another is seen to be utterly
untenable.

Were it possible to carry the Socialist programme
with a rush we could afford to say : " Let personal
and domestic considerations go for next to nothing.
Since in a few short years we shall have compassed
the Revolution, let dignity, decorum, the comfort and
peace of mind of ourselves and our families look after
themselves meanwhile. When the supreme effort has
been crowned with success we can make amends for
present neglect , and even if we cannot, the abiding
social result will justify the temporary personal
sacrifice." Were public opinion solidly with us, the
private character of our spokesmen and organisers
need only be taken into account if it interfered with
the proper discharge of their duty towards the movement. But public opinion is not solidly with us, nor
is the great body of constructive change which we
call Socialism to be carried with a rush. The Social
Revolution will come in its own good time and in its
own way; and in the meantime public opinion is critical
rather than sympathetic ; and our movement is judged
by the general character of its adherents. What we
find is that if in a certain town the movement be

taken up at the outset by the better class of workers, with a sprinkling of the middle and lower-middle class, like attracts like, and the m ivement, standing moderately well in the public estimation, goes forward from one success to another ; but let Socialism be taken up by the rougher type of the rough-and-tumble Socialist, and, so far as that centre is concerned, it will never get much beyond fighting the police, with unemployed agitations and deputations to the authorities ending in smoke of indignant oratory. We may depend upon it that moral improvement is not only desirable for its own sake, but is an indispensable condition to the success of Socialism as a public movement and policy.

But the theory held, perhaps more or less vaguely, by the non-moral Socialists is, nevertheless, not without foundation. They can see that many a careful and prudent workman, husband, and father is at the same time an utterly foolish and dangerous citizen, persistently using his civic powers in opposition to social progress and civilisation. On the other hand, they can see the rough-and-tumble Socialist, much absent from home, frequently out of employment because of his economic rebelliousness, free with his money because full of the spirit of comradeship, and frequently called upon to dip into his wages for contributions towards election expenses, club debts, and on behalf of industrial victims—they can see that this same Socialist may be the very salt of civic life, keeping his little local share of a great movement going, unearthing and exposing abuses, contesting obscure rights, and contributing his quota to general positive progress, while the " respectable householder " passes disdainfully by, full of that severe individualism which the average man calls minding his own business. All this the non-moral Socialist can see; and if the practice of morality meant that we were all to behave like the "respectable householder," there would indeed be no alternative for Socialists but to embrace the non-moral view of Socialism.

But the practice of the "respectable householder" no more represents good conduct than does the behaviour of the rough-and-tumble Socialist. The one is more foolish with his Individualism than the other is with his Socialism. The right lies, as ever, in a golden mean—in a due combination of the domestic and "self-regarding" virtues with the zealous civism and comradeship of the good Socialist. The prime defect of both characters lies in their onesidedness, in the fact that with them prejudices, shibboleths, abstractions stand in the way of questions being decided on their merits. Without being any the less a good husband, father, and workman, the "respectable householder" might at least give his vote to the Socialist candidate at election times, while the enthusiastic Socialist proletaire might even be a more efficient propagandist and general worker for the cause if he would spend more time at home, reading and thinking in the company of his wife and children, if he would go less frequently to the club and to opposition meetings, and if he would insist on the intellectual fare supplied from the lecture platform being more catholic and less stereotyped.

What one sees is the same men attending the club rooms night after night, sweeping, dusting, serving at

the bar, selling tea and tobacco, or wrangling in committee over ways and means; and it becomes impossible to shirk the question: Does the club exist for
these men or do they exist for the club? Outside of
London the movement in England is swamped with
machinery; the mental and consequently the moral
training of our members is neglected; and the complaint on every hand is that no new lecturers are added
to the list. The young men who ought to be attending
classes, studying history, economics, physical science,
and general literature, who ought to be writing letters
to the newspapers, and invading the Mutual Improvement Societies with carefully written papers—these
same young men are making forms, a table, and a
platform for the loft in which the branch meetings are
held, they are tacking calico over the uneven walls and
bare rafters to keep out the draughts and make the
place look a little less like a barn, or they are looking
after the stock of ærated waters. In the early days of
the movement every man was a propagandist; and
among a dozen persons meeting once a week and
reading papers to one another there was more intellectual growth than in branches with hundreds of
members to-day. Our lecturers mostly date their
connection with the movement from the time of which
I speak; and many of them never would have become
lecturers if they had grown up in the atmosphere of
present-day Socialism. Sitting weekly at the feet of
some peripatetic Gamaliel, our members acquire the
idea that lecturing is a vocation by itself, and that it is
not for them to aspire to speak to their fellows in
public. It does not seem to occur to most of us that

men who are not fit for propaganda are not fit to be returned to public bodies. A great deal more of tact and ability are required for the doing of good work in an assembly where you are in a despised and hated minority than for speaking acceptably to an audience mainly composed of friends and sympathisers. The progress of Socialist representation is thus largely dependent on the intellectual growth of the Socialists themselves.

In such circumstances one might give much worse advice than the following :— Abandon your club premises, with their meanness and makeshift ; get away from the beer-ringed tables, the cards and billiards, the sawdusty spittoons, overflowing with burnt matches ; hold fewer perfunctory meetings ; meet in well-appointed halls rented only for the nights on which they are wanted ; hold your committee meetings in members' houses if suitable committee rooms cannot be rented. But if you have funds enough to enable you to secure really decent club premises, and members enough to keep the work going, by all means have a clubhouse ; and let every night of the week see something going on in it for the education of your members. Working men have mostly left school before they realise the use and meaning of what the teacher tried to teach them, and, while they will not attend the ordinary night-school, they would not be so averse to attending classes largely made up of grown men and taught by those of their own class. And so, provided always you have men enough to do the work without undue sacrifice on their part, the clubs might have French classes, economic circles, and circles for the reading of history, in the winter time; they might have classes of domestic economy and house decoration for the women; while during the summer months rambling parties might be formed for the study of botany, geology, and natural history. And, finally, whether the branch be large or small, there ought to be at least one esoteric lecture for your own members once a week. By such means, carried into practice in a serious and spirited manner, it ought to be possible to so intellectualise and moralise the movement as to raise up, among other things, a perfect plethora of propagandists, who should fairly jostle one another for a chance of communicating to others that which they are proud to have learned themselves. The desire to teach, to expound, is natural and widely-diffused; and it is simply the want of knowledge and of seriousness about intellectual things that prevents the man of good natural parts from becoming a propagandist. If any one is inclined to doubt the dialectical ability of the average English Socialist, all he need do is to attend a few branch business meetings. The rhetorical fire and keen logic he will hear expended upon trifling details of procedure ought to settle his doubt once for all.

But, it may be asked, what has all this to do with present possibilities of moral improvement? Well, the difficulty, the impossibility perhaps, of *compelling* moral improvement by direct means has already been pointed out; and the means of *inducing* moral improvement—indirect, roundabout as they must necessarily be—may not at first thought seem to have much relation to the end in view. But I have tried to show by

M

example that, irrespective of economic conditions, men and women have a certain degree of control over their immediate physical and social environment, and that intellectual culture—that prime promoter of moral culture—despite the difficulties with which it is beset, is still not wholly beyond the reach of the wage-labourer. Sometimes an apparently slight influence for good in the surroundings of the individual becomes the medium of radical personal improvement. Have we not all known cases of one member of a loose-living household growing up a quite different being from his or her parents and brothers and sisters, sober amidst drunkards, decent and thoughtful amidst turbulence, folly, and reckless self-indulgence ; and do we not also know that this striking moral superiority is frequently brought about, not so much by original mental superiority as by seemingly slight and fortuitous external causes—friendships casually formed outside the family circle, a hobby or interest developed in youth, a different workshop " set," a sweetheart in whose home life is decorous, sociable, and cheerful ? The endeavour of humanity after righteousness (if we must use theological words) reminds us of plants we have seen in dark and dank corners of a garden struggling up through the overgrowth towards the one speck of light visible in their sunless coverts.

But there is a possibility of underrating the importance of teaching in connection with morals. As continual dropping wears away a stone, surely the regular insistence on right conduct must colour the lives of those who come within the influence of such teaching. If a theological superstition grossly at variance with reason and experience can by mere reiteration be made to have the force of second nature with grown men and women, surely precepts supported by the plain, observable facts of life ought to be capable of acquiring by similar means a similar power.

We Socialists have assumed a responsibility in connection with morals of which we do not always seem to be conscious. We have drawn the sword against the recognised moral teachers of the people. We have stigmatised as blind guides those to whom our hearers have hitherto looked for instruction on the conduct of life; and our condemnation has not fallen upon deaf ears. But have we supplied the place of those whose authority we have so rudely shaken?

The sensible house-mother, tired out with the worry of a week's domestic cares, the decent artisan or small shopkeeper seeking a change from the concerns of the workshop and "business," in which they have brushed up against human nature at its worst, are surely entitled to something of the nature of solace and stimulus and instruction on the one day of the week which is their own. Do they get these things at the average Socialist meeting? I dare not say they do. " The cities of the Commune and the glorious time to be" (as the song-writer has it) are doubtless something to think of, something to live and hope and work for. But is not the consolation of a wholly just and gracious life somewhere in the future, even if our lecturers dealt much and often with it—is it not consolation at a somewhat long range, especially if you have been listening to the tidings for many years, during which your own life has not undergone any

appreciable change for the better ?   And our lecturers
do not deal much and often with the promising future.
Their theme is more commonly the ugly and hateful
present.   And they contrive to make it *so* ugly and *so*
hateful that their scorn and ridicule and relentlessly
cynical logic must sometimes act like salt in the sores
of the buffeted men and women who listen to them.
When one hears a speaker roundly explaining the
motives of capitalists and politicians in terms of the
lowest self-interest, instead of joining in the laugh
provoked by his cynical wit, one sometimes feels inclined to say, in the spirit of Uncle Toby, " Well, if
what you say be true I am very sorry for it."   However
necessary plain speaking may be in addressing those
who are still without the gate, the initiated get restive
under persistent cynicism.

The men and women of whom I have been speaking
already think badly of human nature, are tired of
human nature as they mostly see it, are heartily sick
of the cash nexus, the greed of the money-getter, the
tricks of trade, and all the seaminess of that side of life
which has insisted on thrusting itself on their notice
during the week.   They would fain see the other side,
would fain hear about something that would make
them forget their unpleasant thoughts, were it only
for an hour, something that would send them back to
their drudgery with more of hope and cheerfulness.   It
is not that they desire illusions.   They only wish to
see both sides of " things as they are,"   They know
that there has been a vast amount of heroism and self-
sacrifice, of patient, plodding, and ultimately successful
work on behalf of human kind in the past, and that all

the acts and relations of even landlords and capitalists
are not to be accounted for in terms of the lowest self-
interest. If these men and women would express in
words the standpoint and the longings which they
have perhaps never defined to themselves they would
say something like this : " That landlordism and
capitalism are great historical wrongs, and must give
way to collective ownership in the means of life, with
political and economic equality as between man and
man—of all this I am, and have long been, quite
satisfied. But these things represent a public policy
for society in its corporate capacity, whereas I am ' a
simple, separate person,' having my own individual
life to live, and what I ask is : What have you to say
to me that will make me braver, wiser, more cheerful,
charitable, and useful in the life I have to live here
and now ? On the conduct of life you ought to have
at least as good counsel to give as the priest or the
parson ; and if you have, we are willing to do without
the soothing and comforting effects of the church
music, the ' dim religious light,' the rounded periods
of the cultured preacher, the literary charm of the
hymns and the lessons for the day, and the solemn
impressiveness of church architecture, that

> " ' Art where most magnificent appears
> The little builder man.' "

That, I fancy, would be something like the claim. If
our lecturers are prepared to give us thoughts of fresh
and living interest to turn over in our minds during
the week we may well be content to dispense with a
ceremonial and surroundings which, however gracious

they may be to our emotional nature, are bound up with doctrines which offend our sense of right and reason.

I am satisfied that these needs exist in the minds of many Socialists, and in the minds of many who would be drawn into our movement if we sufficiently catered for those needs ; and it is because of this that I insist on the weekly " esoteric lecture " to our members. And I have dealt throughout with the intellectual and moral improvement of Socialists, because I am ambitious enough to believe that the moral improvement of society in general should largely emanate from the centres of Socialist influence and from the exponents by voice and pen of ˟ocialistic philosophy.

So far, then, we have not got much beyond the means, primarily, of intellectual improvement. But that of itself is not a little. In the opening chapter the inseparableness of mental and moral culture was pointed out. In subsequent chapters the reasons for good conduct were given in some detail, and an effort was made to prove the utility, the necessity, and the admirableness of such virtues as chastity, charity, cheerfulness, courage, truthfulness, honesty, diligence, public spiritedness. These virtues—and especially those of truthfulness and honesty—may not be attainable in their fulness under the unfavourable conditions of present-day life ; but it is incredible that moral evolution should have reached its *ne plus ultra*, under the conditions, in this year of grace 1897. Surely we are not reduced to the necessity of waiting for a substantial improvement in the economic conditions before we can perform any further sloughing off of anti-social

tendencies. Within the period of commercial individualism we can see that considerable moral improvement has taken place. The hard drinking, the loud
vulgar talk, interspersed with a profusion of oaths,
which distinguished the " man of quality " in the early
part of the century, would not be tolerated to-day.
Executions are no longer regarded as galas, but are
carried out in the privacy of a prison, as if we were
ashamed of punishing with murder the crime of
murder. The abolition of chattel slavery and the
more humane feeling shown in connection with the
treatment of the sick poor and the operatives in
factories show that, side by side with the intensifica-
tion of economic individualism, a process of moral
improvement goes on. A glance through the pages
of Evelyn and Pepys, those faithful reflectors of the
every-day life and manners of their time, will sufficiently
indicate the wide moral gulf which divides the life of
to-day from the time in which society dames received
their gentlemen visitors in their bedrooms as a matter
of course, while they sat up in bed to sip their
chocolate. And yet they had private property in land
and capital in the reigns of Charles II. and "good
Queen Anne." Even if economic change were not, as
it is, going on continually, the generations now living
will advance the standard in the domain of morals
just as surely as previous generations have done.

Few things can be more stagnantly anti-social than
the belief that morally all is as well as can be with
us ; that we are " as good as our neighbours " ; that,
having exhausted the possibilities of moral achievement under the conditions, we can afford to take our

ease.   Self-righteous contentment is as dangerous in the sphere of personal ethics as it is in the sphere of social ethics.

In spite of the tyranny of economic conditions, the poorest of us are left with a measure of choice as to our physical environment—the town or district or street in which we shall live   We have equally some choice as to our immediate moral and intellectual environment—our neighbours, friends, associates.   If we cannot keep the company of the best and wisest in the flesh, we can be bosom friends with them in the spirit ; for that great civiliser literature makes us the social equals and intellectual companions, not only of the mighty living, but of the immortal dead.   Thus we can modify the surroundings and purify the atmosphere in which character is subtly built up.   Without Pharisaical Philistinism, we may through all our public and private work cherish a steady regard for whatso-ever things are true and honourable and just and pure and lovely and of good report, remembering always the words of the epigraph which heads this chapter :   " If our cherished ideal of life contradicts and excludes evil tendencies in thought or action our ways of life will do so too; and social and pleasant ways of life are con-tagious. . .   . Ideals are not only for the life to come [either in this world or another]: they are the salva-vation of the life that now is when they are held in the noble and steadfast mind."

[THE END.]

APPENDIX.

A.—BAIN ON THE STERILITY OF ABSTRACT PRINCIPLES
IN ETHICS.

THOSE who have experienced the pleasure of having
their ideas unexpectedly confirmed by a great
authority will understand how the present writer felt
on turning, after the preceding chapters were written,
to Dr. Bain's " Mental and Moral Science," and
finding the following passages advocating the treatment of ethics here adopted :

If we recall some of the great questions of practical life that
have divided the opinions of mankind we shall find that mere
Intuition is helpless to decide them.

Moral right and wrong is not so much a simple, indivisible
property as an extensive code of regulations which cannot even
be understood without a certain maturity of the intelligence.

It is not possible to sum up the whole field of moral right and
wrong so as to bring it within the scope of a single limited
perception, like the perception of resistance or of colour. In
regard to some of the alleged intuitions at the foundation of our
knowledge, as for example time and space, there is a comparative
simplicity and unity rendering their innate origin less disputable.
No such simplicity can be assigned in the region of duty.

After the subject of morals has been studied in the detail it has
indeed been found practicable to comprise the whole, by a kind
of generalisation, in one comprehensive recognition of regard to
our fellows. But, in the first place, this is far from a primitive
or an intuitive suggestion of the mind. It came at a late stage
of human history, and is even regarded as a part of Revelation.
In the second place, this high generality must be accompanied
with detailed applications to particular cases and circumstances.

Life is full of conflicting demands, and there must be special rules to adjust these various demands.   We have to be told that country is greater than family; that temporary interests are to succumb to more enduring, and so on.

Morals is properly considered as a wide-ranging science, having a variety of heads full of difficulty, and demanding minute consideration.   The subject of Justice has nothing simple but the abstract statement—giving each one their [sic] due; before that can be applied we must ascertain what is each person's due, which introduces complex questions of relative merit, far transcending the sphere of intuition.

If any part of morals had the simplicity of an instinct it would be regard to truth.   The difference between truth and falsehood might almost be regarded as a primitive susceptibility, like the difference between light and dark, between resistance and non-resistance.   That each person should say what is, instead of what is not, may well seem a primitive and natural impulse.   In circumstances of perfect indifference, this would be the obvious and usual course of conduct, being, like the straight line, the shortest distance between two points.   Let a motive arise, however, in favour of the lie, and there is nothing to insure the truth.   Reference must be made to other parts of the mind, from which counter-motives may be furnished ; and the intuition in favour of Truth, not being able to support itself, has to repose on the general foundation of all virtue, the instituted recognition of the claims of others.— " Mental and Moral Science," II., 451-2.

It is perhaps to be regretted that Dr. Bain should not have given us a work on the lines he himself indicates.

B.—The Subjection of Women.

The subjection of women now seems in some quarters to be seriously questioned, and, as it happens, in precisely that connection where it is, indirectly, most manifest—namely, the spirit in which the law is administered. That the law as affecting the position of woman in the relation of the sexes is frequently strained in her favour, will be regarded by most people as a tacit admission that her general social status is in itself unfair. This is not the place in which to open the whole question of the position of women, and until the anti-women's-righters (for want of a better name) have made out a stronger case, there is no great necessity for raising so large a question. I submit, however, that in the following respects women are under subjection :

(1) Physically and mentally man as a rule is the stronger, and this always counts enormously in direct personal relations. Practically, whatever the law may say on the matter, the man may commit rape on the woman. Practically, whatever the law may say, a man may beat his wife. Practically, whatever the law may say, the man may, and frequently does, starve his wife and children and spend his money outside of the home. For one woman who will go into court and lay bare the whole anatomy of her domestic skeleton, ninety-nine will suffer in silence. To compile a volume of the cases where women have

been shrews, or drunkards, or unfaithful is pure literary exaggeration and the merest special pleading.

(2) Politically woman is subject to man. She has no vote for members of the Legislature. The fact that she has all the franchises except the Parliamentary franchise counts for comparatively little, since Parliament can take all her political power from her, and has the making, as apart from the administration, of the law as well.

(3) Economically women are subject to the physical sex disability of weakness and the regular periodical ailments connected with menstruation. Men have improved their economic position by combination and legislation. Women, as already stated, have no Parliamentary vote, and can only exercise an indirect and uncertain influence on legislation; while effective combination is rendered almost impossible by the nature of woman's position as a worker. In the industrial field she is merely a probationer, earning or partially earning her own livelihood only until she marries, and never regarding work and trade organisation seriously as that which is to be the vocation of a lifetime. For the rest, employers refuse for various reasons to pay women the same wages as they give to men, and the men refuse to admit women as members of their trade unions because they are unable to command the rates of pay. Thus women have neither much opportunity nor any very strong inducement to escape the economic subjection.

The chief cause of woman's subjection is her relative physical and mental weakness, and while woman remains woman she will, like all female animals, have this disability to contend with. That a feeling of chivalry on the part of judges and juries should incline them to give her the advantage in the administration of the law, and that the law itself should favour women, are both natural and inevitable. We will rather be generous than just to women though, apart from the fact that generosity, like charity, is sometimes an inadequate substitute for justice, strict justice alone can never compensate women for her necessary sex disadvantages. It is a physiological fact and law that the sustenance which in a man goes to nourish the brain and the biceps, in a woman goes to nourish the organs of generation and lactation, and this whether she bears children or not. The Amazonian woman is in the most literal sense an unsexed woman, though even at that she never can and never could develop the strength of a man similarly trained and environed. No law of adaptation could enable woman, by changing her habits of life, to escape the penalties of sex.